FINANCIAL INSTITUTIONS AND SERVICES

THE DODD-FRANK ACT

RULEMAKING COORDINATION AND IMPACT OF RULES

FINANCIAL INSTITUTIONS AND SERVICES

Additional books in this series can be found on Nova's website under the Series tab.

Additional E-books in this series can be found on Nova's website under the E-book tab.

FINANCIAL INSTITUTIONS AND SERVICES

THE DODD-FRANK ACT

RULEMAKING COORDINATION AND IMPACT OF RULES

CANDACE EDMONDS
EDITOR

nova publishers
New York

For permission to use material from this book please contact us:
Telephone 631-231-7269; Fax 631-231-8175
Web Site: http://www.novapublishers.com

Library of Congress Cataloging-in-Publication Data

ISBN: 978-1-62618-050-5

Published by Nova Science Publishers, Inc. † New York

CONTENTS

Preface		**vii**
Chapter 1	Dodd-Frank Act: Agencies' Efforts to Analyze and Coordinate Their Rules *United States Government Accountability Office*	**1**
Chapter 2	The Dodd-Frank Wall Street Reform and Consumer Protection Act: Issues and Summary *Baird Webel*	**117**
Index		**149**

PREFACE

The Dodd-Frank Act requires or authorizes various federal agencies to issue hundreds of rules to implement reforms intended to strengthen the financial services industry. This book examines the regulatory analyses federal agencies performed for rules issued pursuant to the Dodd-Frank Act and how the agencies consulted with each other in implementing the final rules to avoid duplication or conflicts. Most Dodd-Frank Act regulations have not been finalized or in place for sufficient time for their full impacts to materialize. Recognizing these and other limitations, the Government Accountability Office (GAO) took a multipronged approach to assess the impact of some of the act's provisions and rules, with an initial focus on the act's systemic risk goals.

Chapter 1 - The Dodd-Frank Act requires or authorizes various federal agencies to issue hundreds of rules to implement reforms intended to strengthen the financial services industry. GAO is required to annually study financial services regulations. This report examines (1) the regulatory analyses federal agencies performed for rules issued pursuant to the Dodd-Frank Act; (2) how the agencies consulted with each other in implementing the final rules to avoid duplication or conflicts; and (3) what is known about the impact of the Dodd-Frank Act rules. GAO identified 66 final Dodd-Frank Act rules in effect between July 21, 2011, and July 23, 2012. GAO examined the regulatory analyses for the 54 regulations that were substantive and thus required regulatory analyses; conducted case studies on the regulatory analyses for 4 of the 19 major rules; conducted case studies on interagency coordination for 3 other rules; and developed indicators to assess the impact of the act's systemic risk provisions and regulations.

Chapter 2 - Beginning in 2007, U.S. financial conditions deteriorated, leading to the near collapse of the U.S. financial system in September 2008. Major banks, insurers, government-sponsored enterprises, and investment banks either failed or required hundreds of billions in federal support to continue functioning. Households were hit hard by drops in the prices of real estate and financial assets, and by a sharp rise in unemployment. Congress responded to the crisis by enacting the most comprehensive financial reform legislation since the 1930s.

Treasury Secretary Timothy Geithner issued a reform plan in the summer of 2009, which served as a template for legislation in both the House and Senate. House committees reported a number of bills on an issue-by-issue basis, which were then consolidated into a comprehensive bill, the Wall Street Reform and Consumer Protection Act of 2009 (H.R. 4173). H.R. 4173, as passed by the House on December 11, 2009, contained elements of H.R. 1728, H.R. 2571, H.R. 2609, H.R. 3126, H.R. 3269, H.R. 3817, H.R. 3818, H.R. 3890, and H.R. 3996. On May 20, 2010, the Senate passed H.R. 4173, after substituting the text of Senator Christopher Dodd's bill, the Restoring American Financial Stability Act of 2010 (S. 3217), as amended. Following a conference committee, the House accepted changes to H.R. 4173, now titled the Dodd-Frank Wall Street Reform and Consumer Protection Act, on June 30, 2010, and the Senate followed suit on July 15, 2010. President Obama signed the bill, now P.L. 111-203, on July 21, 2010.

Perhaps the major issue in financial reform has been how to address the systemic fragility that was revealed by the crisis. The Dodd-Frank Act creates a new regulatory umbrella group chaired by the Treasury Secretary—the Financial Stability Oversight Council—with authority to designate certain financial firms as "systemically significant" and subjecting them to increased prudential regulation, including limits on leverage, heightened capital standards, and restrictions on certain forms of risky trading. These firms will also be subject to a special resolution process similar to that used in the past to address failing depository institutions.

Other aspects of financial reform address particular sectors of the financial system or selected classes of market participants. The Dodd-Frank Act consolidates consumer protection responsibilities in a new Bureau of Consumer Financial Protection within the Federal Reserve. The act consolidates bank regulation by merging the Office of Thrift Supervision (OTS) into the Office of the Comptroller of the Currency (OCC). It requires more derivatives to be cleared and traded through regulated exchanges, and it mandates reporting for derivatives that remain in the over-the-counter market.

Hedge funds have new reporting and registration requirements. Credit rating agencies are subject to greater disclosure and legal liability provisions, and references to credit ratings will be removed from statute and regulation. A federal office is created to collect insurance information. Executive compensation and securitization reforms attempt to reduce incentives to take excessive risks. Intermediaries who provide investment advice to retail investors and municipalities may be subject to a fiduciary duty. The Federal Reserve's emergency authority is amended and its activities are subject to greater public disclosure and oversight by the Government Accountability Office (GAO).

This report reviews issues related to financial regulation and provides brief descriptions of major provisions of the Dodd-Frank Act.

In: The Dodd-Frank Act
Editor: Candace Edmonds
ISBN: 978-1-62618-050-5

Chapter 1

DODD-FRANK ACT: AGENCIES' EFFORTS TO ANALYZE AND COORDINATE THEIR RULES*

United States Government Accountability Office

WHY GAO DID THIS STUDY

The Dodd-Frank Act requires or authorizes various federal agencies to issue hundreds of rules to implement reforms intended to strengthen the financial services industry. GAO is required to annually study financial services regulations. This report examines (1) the regulatory analyses federal agencies performed for rules issued pursuant to the Dodd-Frank Act; (2) how the agencies consulted with each other in implementing the final rules to avoid duplication or conflicts; and (3) what is known about the impact of the Dodd-Frank Act rules. GAO identified 66 final Dodd-Frank Act rules in effect between July 21, 2011, and July 23, 2012. GAO examined the regulatory analyses for the 54 regulations that were substantive and thus required regulatory analyses; conducted case studies on the regulatory analyses for 4 of the 19 major rules; conducted case studies on interagency coordination for 3 other rules; and developed indicators to assess the impact of the act's systemic risk provisions and regulations.

---

* This is an edited, reformatted and augmented version of the Highlights of GAO-13-101, a report to congressional addressees, dated December 2012.

What GAO Recommends

GAO is not making new recommendations in this report but reiterates its 2011 recommendations that the federal financial regulators more fully incorporate OMB's guidance into their rulemaking policies and that FSOC work with federal financial regulators to establish formal interagency coordination policies for rulemaking. The agencies provided written and technical comments on a draft of this report, and neither agreed nor disagreed with the report's findings.

What GAO Found

Federal agencies conducted the regulatory analyses required by various federal statutes for all 54 regulations issued pursuant to the Dodd-Frank Wall Street Reform and Consumer Protection Act (Dodd-Frank Act) that GAO reviewed. As part of their analyses, the agencies generally considered, but typically did not quantify or monetize, the benefits and costs of these rules. Most of the federal financial regulators, as independent regulatory agencies, are not subject to executive orders that require comprehensive benefit-cost analysis in accordance with guidance issued by the Office of Management and Budget (OMB). Although most financial regulators are not required to follow OMB's guidance, they told GAO that they attempt to follow it in principle or spirit. GAO's review of selected rules found that regulators did not consistently follow key elements of the OMB guidance in their regulatory analyses. For example, while some regulators identified the benefits and costs of their chosen regulatory approach in proposed rules, they did not evaluate their chosen approach compared to the benefits and costs of alternative approaches. GAO previously recommended that regulators more fully incorporate the OMB guidance into their rulemaking policies, and the Office of Comptroller of the Currency and the Securities and Exchange Commission have done so. By not more closely following OMB's guidance, other financial regulators continue to miss an opportunity to improve their analyses.

Federal financial agencies continue to coordinate on rulemakings informally in order to reduce duplication and overlap in regulations and for other purposes, but interagency coordination does not necessarily eliminate the potential for differences in related rules. Agencies coordinated on 19 of the 54 substantive regulations that GAO reviewed. For most of the 19 regulations, the

Dodd-Frank Act required the agencies to coordinate, but agencies also voluntarily coordinated with other U.S. and international regulators on some of their rulemakings. According to the regulators, most interagency coordination is informal and conducted at the staff level. GAO's review of selected rules shows that differences between related rules may remain even when coordination occurs. According to regulators, such differences may result from differences in their jurisdictions or the markets. Finally, the Financial Stability Oversight Council (FSOC) has not yet implemented GAO's previous recommendation to work with regulators to establish formal interagency coordination policies.

Most Dodd-Frank Act regulations have not been finalized or in place for sufficient time for their full impacts to materialize. Recognizing these and other limitations, GAO took a multipronged approach to assess the impact of some of the act's provisions and rules, with an initial focus on the act's systemic risk goals. First, GAO developed indicators to monitor changes in certain characteristics of U.S. bank holding companies subject to enhanced prudential regulation under the Dodd-Frank Act (U.S. bank SIFIs). Although the indicators do not identify causal links between their changes and the act—and many other factors can affect SIFIs—some indicators suggest that since 2010 U.S. bank SIFIs, on average, have decreased their leverage and enhanced their liquidity. Second, empirical results of GAO's regression analysis suggest that, to date, the act may have had little effect on U.S. bank SIFIs' funding costs but may have helped improve their safety and soundness. GAO plans to update its analyses in future reports, including adding indicators for other Dodd-Frank Act provisions and regulations.

ABBREVIATIONS

APA	Administrative Procedure Act
ABS	asset-backed security
CCAR	Comprehensive Capital and Analysis Review
CFPB	Consumer Financial Protection Bureau
CFTC	Commodity Futures Trading Commission
CRA	Congressional Review Act
DCI	data collection instrument
EFTA	Electronic Fund Transfer Act
EO	Executive Order
FDIC	Federal Deposit Insurance Corporation

FSB	Financial Stability Board
FSOC	Financial Stability Oversight Council
GDP	gross domestic product
G-SIB	globally systemically important bank
NCUA	National Credit Union Administration
OCC	Office of the Comptroller of the Currency
OMB	Office of Management and Budget
OFR	Office of Financial Research
PIN	personal identification number
PRA	Paperwork Reduction Act
RFA	Regulatory Flexibility Act
SCAP	Supervisory Capital Assessment Program
SEC	Securities and Exchange Commission
SIFI	systematically important financial institutions
SRO	self-regulatory organization
TARP	Troubled Asset Relief Program
TSR	total absolute shareholder return

December 18, 2012

Congressional Addressees

The 2007-2009 financial crisis created major disruptions in significant parts of the U.S. financial system and threatened the solvency of some large financial institutions, prompting the federal government to take extraordinary steps to moderate the adverse economic impacts. In response to the crisis, Congress passed the Dodd-Frank Wall Street Reform and Consumer Protection Act (Dodd-Frank Act) in 2010, which includes numerous reforms to strengthen oversight of financial services firms and consolidate certain consumer protection responsibilities in the Bureau of Consumer Financial Protection, commonly known as the Consumer Financial Protection Bureau (CFPB).[1] The act requires or authorizes various federal agencies to issue hundreds of regulations to implement its reforms. As agencies have turned their attention to implementing these requirements, some industry associations and others have raised concerns about the potential impact of the regulations, individually and cumulatively, on financial markets and financial and nonfinancial institutions.

Agencies can anticipate and evaluate the consequences of their regulations through regulatory analysis, which provides a formal way of organizing evidence that can help in understanding potential effects of new regulations. Benefit-cost analysis, the primary tool used for regulatory analysis, helps to identify the regulatory alternatives with the greatest net benefits. We, along with the Office of Management and Budget (OMB) and others, have identified benefit-cost analysis as a useful tool that can inform decision making. The systematic process of determining benefits and costs helps decision makers organize and evaluate information about, and identify trade-offs among, alternatives. Because of the merits of benefit-cost analysis, many agencies are directed by statute or executive order to conduct such analysis as part of rulemaking. For example, Executive Order 12,866 (E.O. 12,866) requires executive agencies to assess anticipated costs and benefits not only of the proposed regulatory action but also of any alternatives.[2] However, this order does not apply to independent regulatory agencies, including the banking, futures, and securities regulators (federal financial regulators).[3]

Section 1573(a) of the Department of Defense and Full-Year Continuing Appropriations Act of 2011 amends the Dodd-Frank Act and directs GAO to conduct an annual study of financial services regulations, including those of CFPB.[4] In November 2011, we issued our first report under this mandate.[5] Since that report, we have continued to monitor the development of rules and regulations related to the Dodd-Frank Act. Specifically, this report examines

- the regulatory analyses, including benefit-cost analyses, that federal financial regulators have performed to assess the potential impact of selected final rules issued pursuant to the Dodd-Frank Act;
- how federal financial regulators consulted with each other in implementing selected final rules issued pursuant to the Dodd-Frank Act to avoid duplication or conflicts; and
- what is known about the impact of the Dodd-Frank Act regulations on the financial marketplace.

To address the first objective, we reviewed all final rules—a total of 66—that were issued pursuant to the Dodd-Frank Act and became effective between July 21, 2011, and July 23, 2012, to catalogue the regulatory analyses (including benefit-cost analyses) the federal financial regulators conducted.[6] Combined with the 32 rules we identified in our first report, we identified 98 Dodd-Frank Act rules in effect as of July 23, 2012.[7] To assess the regulatory analyses of the agencies, we reviewed the 66 rules that were issued and became effective between July 21, 2011, and July 23, 2012. Of these rules, 54 are substantive regulations while 12 are interpretive rules; general statements of policy; and rules that deal with agency organization, procedure, or practice. Unlike interpretive rules, general statements of policy, and rules that deal with agency organization, procedure, or practice, substantive regulations are subject to the notice-and-comment rulemaking requirements of the Administrative Procedure Act (APA) and generally include some form of regulatory analysis.[8] Thus, our review focused on the 54 substantive regulations for our analysis. Of the 54 regulations, 19 rules were determined by the regulators and OMB to be "major" rules that could have an annual impact on the economy of $100 million or more. For agencies subject to E.O. 12866, such major rules would be considered significant regulatory actions and subject to formal benefit-cost analysis.[9] Three federal financial regulators issued 18 of the 19 major rules: the Board of Governors of the Federal Reserve System (Federal Reserve), Commodity Futures Trading Commission (CFTC), and Securities and Exchange Commission (SEC). In addition, the Department of the Treasury (Treasury), which is subject to E.O. 12,866, issued the other major rule pursuant to the Dodd-Frank Act. We selected four major rules for in-depth review and compared the analyses conducted to the principles outlined in OMB Circular A-4, which provides guidance to federal agencies on the development of regulatory analysis.[10] Within our scope period, the Federal Reserve and Treasury each issued one major rule that we selected. We selected the lone SEC major rule during the period that implemented new statutory authority. CFTC issued several major rules, and we selected a rule based on our discussions with current and former CFTC staff. We interviewed agency staffs and reviewed documentation from the agencies to assess the quality of the benefit-cost or similar analyses. We also reviewed statutes, regulations, agency guidance, and other documentation to identify the analyses federal financial regulators were required to conduct and how the agency intended to conduct them.

To examine interagency coordination among or between federal financial regulators in developing rules, we reviewed the 66 Dodd-Frank rules that were issued and became effective between July 21, 2011, and July 23, 2012, to identify which required interagency coordination and document whether such coordination occurred. We identified 19 rules that required interagency coordination. Of the rules requiring interagency coordination, we selected three for case studies to examine the extent to which and how agencies coordinated to avoid conflict and duplication in rulemaking. We selected the rules to include at least one that two or more regulators jointly issued and at least one that a single regulator issued. We also selected rules to include as many of the federal financial regulators as possible, including the Federal

Reserve, CFTC, SEC, the Office of the Comptroller of the Currency (OCC), and the Federal Deposit Insurance Corporation (FDIC). We interviewed agency staff and reviewed documentation from the agencies to assess the extent to which and how agencies coordinated to avoid conflict and duplication in rulemaking.

To examine the impact of Dodd-Frank Act regulations on the financial marketplace, we took a multipronged approach. We developed a set of indicators to monitor changes in certain characteristics of systemically important financial institutions (SIFI) that might be affected by Dodd-Frank Act regulations.[11] To that end, we reviewed the legislative history of the Dodd-Frank Act, the act itself, related regulations, academic studies, GAO and agency reports, and other relevant documentation. Although changes in the indicators may be suggestive of the impact of the act on SIFIs, the indicators have a number of limitations, including that they do not identify any causal linkages between the act and changes in the indicators. Moreover, factors other than the act affect SIFIs and, thus, the indicators. Additionally, we developed a set of indicators related to the (1) cost of credit provided by bank SIFIs and (2) safety and soundness of bank SIFIs. We used regression analysis to estimate the changes in the indicators of bank SIFIs that may be associated with Dodd-Frank Act provisions and proposed regulations related to the enhanced prudential regulation of these bank holding companies by the Federal Reserve. Our analysis does not differentiate the effects of the act from simultaneous changes in economic conditions or other factors that may affect such companies. We obtained and addressed high-level comments and suggestions on all our indicators from Financial Stability Oversight Council (FSOC) staff and two other market experts. Finally, we analyzed the initial impacts of several major rules that were issued pursuant to the Dodd-Frank Act and have been final for around 1 year or more. As part of that work, we reviewed selected regulations, analyzed available data about the potential impacts of the regulations, and interviewed agency officials and market participants about such impacts. Appendix I contains additional information on our scope and methodology.

We conducted this performance audit from December 2011 to December 2012 in accordance with generally accepted government auditing standards. Those standards require that we plan and perform the audit to obtain sufficient, appropriate evidence to provide a reasonable basis for our findings and conclusions based on our audit objectives. We believe that the evidence obtained provides a reasonable basis for our findings and conclusions based on our audit objectives.

Background

Financial Services Regulation

The U.S. financial regulatory structure is a complex system of multiple federal and state regulators as well as self-regulatory organizations (SRO) that operate largely along functional lines. That is, financial products or activities generally are regulated according to their function, no matter who offers the product or participates in the activity. The functional regulator approach is intended to provide consistency in regulation, focus regulatory restrictions on the relevant functional areas, and avoid the potential need for regulatory agencies to develop expertise in all aspects of financial regulation.

In the banking industry, the specific regulatory configuration depends on the type of charter the banking institution chooses. Charter types for depository institutions include commercial banks, thrifts, and credit unions. These charters may be obtained at the state or federal level. The federal prudential banking regulators—all of which generally may issue regulations and take enforcement actions against industry participants within their jurisdiction—are identified in table 1. In addition, the Dodd-Frank Act created CFPB as an independent bureau within the Federal Reserve System that is responsible for regulating the offering and provision of consumer financial products and services under the federal consumer financial laws. Under the Dodd-Frank Act, at the designated transfer date, certain authority vested in the prudential regulators transferred to CFPB.[12] The securities and futures industries are regulated under a combination of self-regulation (subject to oversight by the appropriate federal regulator) and direct oversight by SEC and CFTC, respectively. SEC oversees the securities industry SROs, and the securities industry as a whole, and is responsible for administering federal securities laws and developing regulations for the industry. SEC's overall mission includes protecting investors; maintaining fair, orderly, and efficient markets; and facilitating capital formation. CFTC oversees the futures industry and its SROs. Under the Dodd-Frank Act, CFTC also has extensive responsibilities for the regulation of swaps and certain entities involved in the swaps markets. CFTC has responsibility for administering federal legislation and developing comprehensive regulations to protect the public from fraud and manipulation, to insure the financial integrity of transactions, and to reduce systemic risk in the marketplace. In addition, the Dodd-Frank Act created FSOC.[13] FSOC's three primary purposes are to identify risks to the financial stability of the United States, promote market discipline, and respond to emerging threats to the stability of the U.S. financial system. FSOC consists of 10 voting members and 5 nonvoting members and is chaired by the Secretary of the Treasury.[14] In consultation with the other FSOC members, the Secretary is responsible for regular consultation with the financial regulatory entities and other appropriate organizations of foreign governments or international organizations.

Table 1. Prudential Regulators and Their Basic Functions

Agency	Basic function
Office of the Comptroller of the Currency	Charters and supervises national banks and federal thrifts.
Board of Governors of the Federal Reserve System	Supervises state-chartered banks that opt to be members of the Federal Reserve System, bank holding companies, thrift holding companies and the nondepository institution subsidiaries of those institutions, and nonbank financial companies designated by the Financial Stability Oversight Council.
Federal Deposit Insurance Corporation	Supervises FDIC-insured state-chartered banks that are not members of the Federal Reserve System, as well as federally insured state savings banks and thrifts; insures the deposits of all banks and thrifts that are approved for federal deposit insurance; and resolves all failed insured banks and thrifts and has been given the authority to resolve large bank holding companies and nonbank financial companies that are subject to supervision by the Board of Governors of the Federal Reserve System and subject to enhanced prudential standards.[a]
National Credit Union Administration	Charters and supervises federally chartered credit unions and insures savings in federal and most state-chartered credit unions.

Source: GAO.

[a] 12 U.S.C. § 5384.

Regulations and Federal Rulemaking

The federal government uses regulation to implement public policy. Section 553 of APA contains requirements for the most common type of federal rulemaking—informal rulemaking or "notice and comment" rulemaking.[15] While there are inter- and intra-agency variations in the informal rulemaking process, federal financial regulators generally share three basic rulemaking steps or phases:

- **Initiation of rulemaking action.** During initiation, agencies gather information that would allow them to determine whether rulemaking is needed and identify potential regulatory options. To gather information on the need for rulemaking and potential regulatory options, agencies may hold meetings with interested parties or issue an advanced notice of proposed rulemaking. At this time, the agencies also will identify the resources needed for the rulemaking and may draft concept documents for agency management that summarize the issues, present the regulatory options, and identify needed resources.
- **Development of proposed rule.** During this phase of the rulemaking process, an agency will draft the notice of proposed rulemaking, including the preamble (which is the portion of the rule that informs the public of the supporting reasons and purpose of the rule) and the rule language. The agency will begin to address analytical and procedural requirements in this phase. The agency provides "interested persons" with an opportunity to comment on the proposed rule, generally for a period of at least 30 days.[16]
- **Development of final rule.** In the third phase, the agency repeats, as needed, the steps used during development of the proposed rule. Once the comment period closes for the proposed rule, the agency either would modify the proposed rule to incorporate comments or address the comments in the final rule release. This phase also includes opportunities for internal and external review. As published in the *Federal Register*, the final rule includes the date on which it becomes effective.

APA's notice and comment procedures exclude certain categories of rules, including interpretative rules; general statements of policy; rules that deal with agency organization, procedure, or practice; or rules for which the agency finds (for good cause) that notice and public comment procedures are impracticable, unnecessary or contrary to the public interest.

Dodd-Frank Act Regulations

Under the Dodd-Frank Act, federal financial regulatory agencies are directed or have the authority to issue hundreds of regulations to implement the act's provisions. In some cases, the act gives the agencies little or no discretion in deciding how to implement the provisions. For instance, the

Dodd-Frank Act made permanent a temporary increase in the FDIC deposit insurance coverage amount ($100,000 to $250,000); therefore, FDIC revised its implementing regulation to conform to the change. However, other rulemaking provisions in the act appear to be discretionary in nature, stating that (1) certain agencies may issue rules to implement particular provisions or that the agencies may issue regulations that they decide are "necessary and appropriate"; or (2) agencies must issue regulations to implement particular provisions but have some level of discretion over the substance of the regulations. As a result, for these rulemaking provisions, the agencies may decide to promulgate rules for some or all of the provisions, and may have broad discretion to decide what these rules will contain and what exemptions, if any, will apply.

In many instances, exemptions to Dodd-Frank Act provisions are encompassed in definitions of certain terms that are broadly established in statute and require clarification through regulation. Persons or entities that meet the regulatory definitions are subject to the provision, and those that do not meet the definitions are not. For example, CFTC and SEC promulgated a regulation that defined the terms "swap dealer," "security- based swap dealer," "major swap participant," "major security-based swap participant," and "eligible contract participant."[17] Persons that do not meet the definitions of these terms may not be subject to the Dodd- Frank Act provisions concerning swaps and security-based swaps, including registration, margin, capital, business conduct, and other requirements. Similarly, FSOC promulgated a regulation and interpretive guidance regarding the specific criteria and analytic framework FSOC would apply in determining whether a nonbank financial company could pose a threat to the financial stability of the United States.[18] Financial firms that are not designated by FSOC, acting pursuant to the statutory standards, would not be subject to enhanced prudential supervision by the Federal Reserve.

Regulatory Analyses Provide Limited Information about Benefits and Costs of Chosen or Alternative Approaches

Federal agencies conducted the regulatory analyses required by various federal statutes for all 54 Dodd-Frank Act regulations that we reviewed. As part of their analyses, the agencies generally considered, but typically did not quantify or monetize, the benefits and costs of these regulations. As independent regulatory agencies, the federal financial regulators are not subject to executive orders that require comprehensive benefit-cost analysis in accordance with guidance issued by OMB. While most financial regulators said that they attempt to follow OMB's guidance in principle or spirit, we found that they did not consistently follow key elements of the guidance in their regulatory analyses. We previously recommended that regulators should more fully incorporate the OMB guidance into their rulemaking policies.

Regulators Were Not Required to Assess Benefits and Costs of Regulatory Alternatives

As part of their rulemakings, federal agencies generally must conduct regulatory analysis pursuant to the Paperwork Reduction Act (PRA) and the Regulatory Flexibility Act (RFA), among other statutes.[19] PRA and RFA require federal agencies to assess various impacts and costs of their rules, but do not require the agencies to formally assess the benefits and costs of alternative regulatory approaches or the reason for selecting one alternative over another. In addition to these requirements, authorizing or other statutes require certain federal financial regulators to consider specific benefits, costs, and impacts of their rulemakings, as the following describes.

- CFTC, under section 15(a) of the Commodity Exchange Act, is required to consider the benefits and costs of its action before promulgating a regulation under the Commodity Exchange Act or issuing certain orders. Section 15(a) further specifies that the benefits and costs shall be evaluated in light of the following five broad areas of market and public concern: (1) protection of market participants and the public; (2) efficiency, competitiveness, and financial integrity of futures markets; (3) price discovery; (4) sound risk-management practices; and (5) other public interest considerations.[20]
- Under the Consumer Financial Protection Act (Title X of the Dodd-Frank Act), CFPB must consider the potential benefits and costs of its rules for consumers and entities that offer or provide consumer financial products and services. These include potential reductions in consumer access to products or services, the impacts on depository institutions with $10 billion or less in assets, as directed by 12 U.S.C. § 5516, and the impacts on consumers in rural areas.[21] In its initial

RFA analysis, CFPB also must describe any projected increase in the cost of credit for small entities and any significant alternatives that would minimize such increases for small entities.[22]

- In addition to the protection of investors, SEC must consider whether a rule will promote efficiency, competition, and capital formation whenever it is engaged in rulemaking and is required to consider or determine whether an action is necessary or appropriate in the public interest.[23] SEC also must consider the impact that any rule promulgated under the Securities Exchange Act would have on competition.[24] This provision states that a rule should not be adopted if it would impose a burden on competition that is not necessary or appropriate to the act's purposes.
- The Electronic Funds Transfer Act (EFTA), as amended by the Dodd-Frank Act, requires the Federal Reserve to prepare an analysis of the economic impact of a specific regulation that considers the costs and benefits to financial institutions, consumers, and other users of electronic fund transfers.[25] The analysis must address the extent to which additional paperwork would be required, the effect upon competition in the provision of electronic banking services among large and small financial institutions, and the availability of such services to different classes of consumers, particularly low-income consumers.

However, like PRA and RFA, none of these authorizing statutes prescribe formal, comprehensive benefit and cost analyses that require the identification and assessment of alternatives.

In contrast, Executive Order 12,866 (E.O. 12,866), supplemented by Executive Order 13,563 (E.O. 13,563), requires covered federal agencies, to the extent permitted by law and where applicable, to (1) assess benefits and costs of available regulatory alternatives and (2) include both quantifiable and qualitative measures of benefits and costs in their analysis, recognizing that some benefits and costs are difficult to quantify.[26] According to OMB, such analysis can enable an agency to learn if the benefits of a rule are likely to justify the costs and discover which of the possible alternatives would yield the greatest net benefit or be the most cost-effective. In 2003, OMB issued Circular A-4 to provide guidance to federal executive agencies on the development of regulatory analysis as required by E.O. 12,866.[27] The guidance defines good regulatory analysis as including a statement of the need for the proposed regulation, an assessment of alternatives, and an evaluation of the benefits and costs of the proposed regulation and the alternatives. It also standardizes the way benefits and costs of federal regulatory actions should be measured and reported. Of the federal agencies included in our review, only FSOC and Treasury are subject to E.O. 12,866. As independent regulatory agencies, the federal financial regulators—CFPB, CFTC, FDIC, the Federal Reserve, OCC, the National Credit Union Administration (NCUA), and SEC—are not subject to E.O. 12,866 and OMB's Circular A-4.[28]

Of the 66 Dodd-Frank Act rules within our scope, 54 regulations were substantive—generally subject to public notice and comment under APA—and required the agencies to conduct regulatory analysis. These rules were issued individually or jointly by CFTC, FDIC, the Federal Reserve, FSOC, NCUA, OCC, SEC, or Treasury.[29] (See app. II for a list of the regulations within the scope of our review.) In examining the regulatory analyses conducted for these 54 regulations, we found the following.

- **Agencies conducted the required regulatory analyses.** The agencies conducted regulatory analysis pursuant to PRA and RFA for all 54 regulations. Agencies also conducted the analyses required under their authorizing statutes. Specifically, CFTC and SEC individually or jointly issued 39 regulations and considered their potential impact, including their benefits and costs in light of each agency's respective public interest considerations.
- **Agencies issued 19 major rules.** Of the 54 regulations that were issued and became effective between July 21, 2011, and July 23, 2012, the agencies identified 19 as being major rules—that is, resulting in or likely to result in a $100 million annual impact on the economy. Specifically, CFTC issued 10 major rules; SEC issued 5 major rules; CFTC and SEC jointly issued 2 major rules; the Federal Reserve issued 1 major rule; and Treasury issued 1 major rule.[30]
- **One of the 19 major rules was subject to E.O. 12866 and its benefit-cost analysis requirement.** Of the agencies that issued major rules, only Treasury is subject to E.O. 12,866, which requires a formal assessment of the benefits and costs of an economically significant rule. Thus, as required, Treasury analyzed the benefits and costs of its proposed major rule.[31]
- **Agencies considered the benefits and/or costs in the majority of their rules, but did not generally quantify them.** As part of their regulatory analyses or in response to public comments received on their proposed rules, the agencies frequently discussed the potential

benefits and costs of their rules. For instance, CFTC and SEC asked for public comments and data on the benefits and costs in all of their proposed rules, and the other regulators generally asked for public comments on the costs and, in many cases, benefits of their proposed rules. For the 54 substantive Dodd-Frank Act regulations that we reviewed, 49 regulations included discussions of potential benefits or costs. The cost discussions primarily were qualitative except for the PRA analysis, which typically included quantitative data (such as hours or dollars spent to comply with paperwork-related requirements). Other potential costs, however, were less frequently quantified. In comparison, the benefit discussions largely were qualitative and framed in terms of the objectives of the rules.

Regulators Generally Developed Selected Major Rules in Ways Consistent with the Principles, but not Certain Key Elements, of the OMB Guidance

Although independent federal financial regulators are not required to follow OMB's Circular A-4 when developing regulations, they told us that they try to follow this guidance in principle or spirit. As discussed in more detail below, we previously found that the policies and procedures of these agencies did not fully reflect OMB guidance and recommended that they incorporate the guidance more fully in their rulemaking policies and procedures.[32] To assess the extent to which the regulators follow Circular A-4, we examined four major rules (see table 2). Specifically, we examined whether the regulators (1) identified the problem to be addressed by the regulation and the significance of the problem; (2) considered alternatives reflecting the range of statutory discretion; and (3) assessed the benefits and costs of the regulation.

While the regulators identified the problem to be addressed in their rule proposals, CFTC, the Federal Reserve, and SEC did not present benefit- cost information in ways consistent with certain key elements of OMB's Circular A-4. For example, CFTC and SEC did not evaluate the benefits and costs of regulatory alternatives they considered for key provisions compared to their chosen approach. Also, because of the lack of data and for other reasons, the agencies generally did not quantitatively analyze the benefits and, to a lesser degree, costs in their rules.

Agencies' approaches for calculating a baseline against which to compare benefits and costs of regulatory alternatives in their analysis varied, and agency staffs told us that the lack of data complicated such efforts.

Table 2. Summary of Four Major Rules Reviewed

Rulemaking	Responsible regulator	Rule synopsis
Real-Time Public Reporting of Swap Transaction Data	CFTC	Provides standards for the method and timing of real-time public reporting; swap transaction and pricing data to be publicly disseminated in real-time; and time delays for public dissemination of swap transaction and pricing data.
Debit Card Interchange Fees and Routing	Federal Reserve	Provides standards for reasonable and proportional interchange transaction fees for electronic debit transactions, exemptions from the interchange transaction fee limitations, prohibitions on evasion and circumvention, prohibitions on payment card network exclusivity arrangements and routing restrictions for debit card transactions, and reporting requirements for debit card issuers and payment card networks.
Securities Whistleblower Incentives and Protections	SEC	Provides for payment of awards, subject to certain limitations and conditions, to whistleblowers who voluntarily provide SEC with original information about a violation of the securities laws that leads to the successful enforcement of an action brought by SEC that results in monetary sanctions exceeding $1,000,000.
Assessment of Fees on Large Bank Holding Companies and Nonbank Financial Companies Supervised by the Federal Reserve Board to Cover the Expenses of the Financial Research Fund	Treasury	Provides standards directing how Treasury will (a) determine which companies will be subject to an assessment fee, (b) estimate the total expenses that are necessary to carry out the activities to be covered by the assessment, (c) determine the assessment fee for each of these companies, and (d) bill and collect the assessment fee from these companies.

Source: GAO summary of information from the Federal Register.

Evaluation of Alternative Approaches in Proposed Rules

Two of the major rules we reviewed did not evaluate alternative approaches for key provisions in their rule proposals, but the final rule releases did evaluate alternatives considered by the agencies. In implementing the Dodd-Frank provisions, the agencies exercised discretion in designing the various requirements that composed their rules, such as defining key terms and determining who will be subject to the regulations and how. In their rule proposals, CFTC and SEC identified alternative approaches for key provisions of their rule proposals. For example, CFTC identified the consolidated tape approach—which is used in the U.S. securities markets to publicly report data on securities—as an alternative method for distributing swap transaction data in real time. SEC considered requiring potential whistleblowers to use in-house complaint and reporting procedures before they make a whistleblower submission to SEC. However, CFTC and SEC generally did not evaluate the benefits and costs of their proposed rules' requirements compared to such alternative requirements. Instead, their rule proposals only presented the proposed set of requirements composing their rules and discussed the potential benefits and costs of their overall regulatory approaches. As part of their proposed rules, CFTC and SEC asked the public for comments on a number of questions, including about possible alternatives to proposed requirements.[33] In their final rules, CFTC and SEC noted that they considered alternatives provided by commenters on the proposed rules and revised their rules, so as to reduce regulatory burden or improve the effectiveness of the rules. This approach generally is consistent with each agency's guidance on regulatory analysis.[34] However, OMB guidance notes that good regulatory analysis is designed to inform the public and other parts of the government of the effects of alternative actions. Without information about the agency's evaluation of the benefits and costs of alternatives for key provisions, interested parties may not have a clear understanding of the assumptions underlying the rule's requirements, which could hinder their ability to comment on proposed rules.

One of the rules we reviewed identified the alternative approaches but did not describe the reasons for choosing one alternative over another in its rule proposal. The Federal Reserve identified several alternative approaches for key provisions in the rule proposal for implementing the interchange fee rule and some of their potential benefits and costs. However, it did not determine which of the alternatives would produce greater net benefits or be more cost-effective. Instead, the Federal Reserve asked the public to comment on which alternatives might be preferable to the others based on several factors, including benefits and costs. Federal Reserve staff told us that they took this approach because it was difficult to predict how market participants would respond to the rule. They said that they had discussions with senior management about alternative approaches and analyzed the costs and benefits of the alternatives, including how alternatives could have different impacts on different market participants, but this information was not contained in the proposed rule. In the final rule, responding to public comments, the Federal Reserve selected one alternative over the other alternatives and provided reasons for the selection. Without information about the rationale for selecting one alternative over another in the proposed rule, interested parties may not know how to effectively gauge the magnitude of the potential effects, which could hinder their ability to comment on the proposed rule.

Only one rule that we reviewed identified and evaluated alternative regulatory approaches. In its rule proposal, Treasury determined that the fee assessment rule was a significant regulatory action under E.O. 12,866 and, thus, conducted a regulatory impact assessment. In its proposal, Treasury identified, evaluated, and discussed several alternative regulatory approaches. Treasury evaluated the impact of alternative approaches on interested parties and selected the approach it viewed as equitable and cost-effective, consistent with the OMB guidance.

Quantitative Analysis of Benefits and Costs of Major Rules

The regulators generally did not quantitatively analyze the benefits and, to a lesser degree, costs of the rules we reviewed. CFTC, the Federal Reserve, and SEC did not quantitatively analyze the benefits of these rules. CFTC and SEC monetized and quantified paperwork-related costs under PRA, but did not quantify any other costs. Federal Reserve staff told us that they monetized some of the direct costs of the debit card interchange fee rule. Specifically, they conducted a survey to determine an average debit card interchange fee in 2009 and used that data to help establish the debit card interchange fee cap under the rule. However, while the debit card interchange fee cap information was included in the proposed rule, measures of revenue loss that could result from the rule were not included.[35] In contrast to the other rules we reviewed, Treasury monetized and quantified some costs of the rule beyond paperwork-related costs. Specifically, Treasury provided a range of estimated assessment amounts that described the approximate size of the transfer from assessed companies to the government.

As we have reported, the difficulty of reliably estimating the costs of regulations to the financial services industry and the nation has long been recognized, and the benefits of regulation generally are regarded as even more difficult to measure. Similarly, Circular A-4 recognizes that some important benefits and costs may be inherently too difficult to quantify or monetize given current data and methods and recommends a careful evaluation of qualitative benefits and costs. All of the rules we reviewed included qualitative descriptions of the potential benefits and costs associated with the rules. The agencies also generally included qualitative information on the nature, timing, likelihood, location, and distribution of the benefits and costs. For instance, in discussing the benefits of the reporting and public dissemination requirements, CFTC stated that it anticipates that the real-time reporting rule "will generate several overarching, if presently unquantifiable, benefits to swaps market participants and the public generally. These include: [i]mprovements in market quality; price discovery; improved risk management; economies of scale and greater efficiencies; and improved regulatory oversight."[36] CFTC then went on to describe the ways in which these benefits might accrue to market participants. However, some of the agencies did not discuss the strengths and limitations of the qualitative information and did not discuss key reasons why the benefits and costs could not be quantified. Also, the regulators did not consistently present analysis of any important uncertainties connected with their regulatory decisions. For instance, the Federal Reserve stated that the potential impacts of the debit card interchange fee rule depended in large part on the reaction of certain market actors to the rule. In contrast, we did not find a discussion of any important uncertainties associated with SEC's whistleblower rules, but SEC staff told us that the inherent uncertainties in making predictions about human behavior was a key reason why it was not possible to engage in a quantitative analysis of the rule. However, we found that the agencies generally based their analyses on the best reasonably available, peer-reviewed economic information. Treasury described certain direct costs associated with complying with the fee assessment rule. Treasury used economic reasoning to identify some benefits or types of benefits associated with the rule, particularly in considering the choice of assessment methodology, which was the area of discretion left by Congress to the agency.

Establishment of Baseline for Analysis

We also found the regulators' approaches for calculating a baseline against which to compare benefits and costs of regulatory approaches varied. OMB's Circular A-4 states that the baseline should be the best assessment of the way the world would look absent the proposed action. In cases where substantial portions of the rule may simply restate statutory requirements that would be self-implementing, Circular A-4 provides for use of a prestatute baseline—that is, the baseline should reflect the status quo before the statute was enacted. However, the guidance further states that if the agency is able to determine where it has discretion in implementing a statute, it can use a post-statute baseline to evaluate the discretionary elements of the action. CFTC and SEC both did not establish post-statute baselines and instead evaluated the benefits and costs of the discretionary elements of their rules in terms of statutory objectives. Specifically, CFTC evaluated each discretionary element of the real-time reporting rule based on whether it met the statutory objectives to reduce risk, increase transparency, and promote market integrity.[37] Similarly, SEC evaluated each discretionary element of the whistleblower protection rule according to four broad objectives based on statutory goals and the nature of public comments.[38] We found that the Federal Reserve generally took this approach in developing the debit card interchange fee rule. In contrast, Treasury, which is subject to E.O. 12,866, used a post-statute baseline to evaluate the discretionary elements of the fee assessment rule. SEC staff said they would have described the analysis somewhat differently under their new economic analysis guidance (discussed below), which directs staff to consider the overall economic impacts, including both those attributable to congressional mandates and those that result from an exercise of discretion. SEC's guidance states that this approach often will allow for a more complete picture of a rule's economic effects, particularly because there are many situations in which it is difficult to distinguish between the mandatory and discretionary components of a rule. Agency staffs told us developing a baseline from which to assess the benefits and costs of what would have happened in the absence of a regulation was complicated by the lack of reliable data to quantify the benefits and costs. For example, CFTC staff told us that they were challenged because little public data were available about the opaque swaps market. Moreover, because the rule created a new regulatory regime, CFTC did not have the data needed for the analysis. Instead, CFTC had to rely on market participants to voluntarily provide it with proprietary data. CFTC staff said that they did receive some proprietary data but that they were incomplete. Similarly, for the whistleblower protection rule, SEC staff said that they asked the public for data in their draft rule but did not receive any. In the absence of data, SEC cited related research in its rule release, but staff noted that they were reluctant to weigh this research too heavily because the programs covered in the research differed in important respects from SEC's program. In addition, Federal Reserve staff said that quantifying the effects of the debit card interchange fee rule was a major challenge because of the lack of data.

Some Agencies' Guidance on Regulatory Analysis Continues to Omit Key Elements of OMB's Regulatory Guidance

Although not subject to E.O. 12,866 and, in turn, OMB Circular A-4, most of the federal regulators told us that they try to follow Circular A-4 in principle or spirit.[39] In our previous review, we found that the policies and procedures of these regulators did not fully reflect OMB guidance and recommended that they incorporate the guidance more fully in their rulemaking policies and procedures. For example, each federal regulator has issued guidance generally explaining how its staff should analyze the benefits and costs of the regulatory approach selected, but unlike the OMB guidance, such guidance generally does not encourage staff to identify and analyze the benefits and costs of available alternative approaches. Since we issued our report, OCC and SEC have revised their guidance, but the other agencies have not yet done so. CFTC last revised its guidance in May 2011, and in May 2012 it signed a Memorandum of Understanding with OMB that allows OMB staff to provide technical assistance to CFTC staff as they consider the benefits and costs of proposed and final rules.[40]

Issued in March 2012, SEC guidance on economic analysis for rulemakings closely follows E.O. 12,866 and Circular A-4.[41] Specifically, SEC's guidance defines the basic elements of good regulatory economic analysis in a manner that closely parallels the elements listed in Circular A-4: (1) a statement of the need for the proposed action; (2) the definition of a baseline against which to measure the likely economic consequences of the proposed regulation; (3) the identification of alternative regulatory approaches; and (4) an evaluation of the benefits and costs—both quantitative and qualitative—of the proposed action and the main alternatives. In addition, the guidance explains these elements and describes the ways rulemaking teams can satisfy each of the elements borrowing directly from Circular A-4. OCC guidance on economic analysis defines the elements included in a full cost-benefit analysis in a similar fashion and includes citations to specific sections of Circular A-4 to guide staff through the application of each element.

For other federal financial regulators, by continuing to omit core elements of OMB Circular A-4, their regulatory guidance may cause staff to overlook or omit such best practices in their regulatory analysis. In turn, the analyses produced may lack information that interested parties (including consumers, investors, and other market participants) could use to make more informed comments on proposed rules. For example, in our review of four major rules, we found that most of the agencies did not consistently discuss how they selected one regulatory alternative over another or assess the potential benefits and costs of available alternatives. Without information about the benefits and costs of alternatives that agencies considered, interested parties may not know which alternatives were considered and the effects of such alternatives, which could hinder their ability to comment on proposed rules. More fully incorporating OMB's guidance into their rulemaking guidance, as we previously recommended, could help agencies produce more robust and transparent rulemakings.

REGULATORS CONTINUE TO COORDINATE INFORMALLY ON RULEMAKINGS, BUT DIFFERENCES AMONG RELATED RULES STILL EXIST

Federal financial regulators have continued to coordinate on rulemakings informally, but coordination may not eliminate the potential for differences in related rules. Regulators have coordinated on 19 of the 54 substantive regulations that we reviewed, in some cases voluntarily coordinating their activities and also extending coordination internationally. According to agency staff, most interagency coordination during rulemaking largely was informal and conducted at the staff level. Differences in rules could remain after interagency coordination, because the rules reflected differences in factors such as regulatory jurisdiction or market or product type. While a few regulators have made progress on developing guidance for interagency coordination during rulemaking, most have not.

Dodd-Frank Act and Regulators Recognize the Importance of Interagency Coordination

Both the Dodd-Frank Act and the federal financial regulators whom we interviewed recognize the importance of interagency coordination during the rulemaking process. In general, coordination during the rulemaking process occurs when two or more regulators jointly engage in activities to reduce duplication and overlap in regulations. Effective coordination could help regulators minimize or eliminate staff and industry burden, administrative costs, conflicting regulations, unintended consequences, and uncertainty among consumers and markets.

Recognizing the importance of coordination, the act imposes specific interagency coordination and consultation requirements and responsibilities on regulators or certain rules. For instance, section 171 (referred to as the Collins Amendment) requires that the appropriate federal banking agencies establish a risk-based capital floor on a consolidated basis.[42] In addition, while section 619 (referred to as the Volcker Rule) does not require the federal banking agencies (FDIC, the Federal Reserve, and OCC) to issue a joint rule together with CFTC and SEC, it requires that they consult and coordinate with each other, in part to better ensure that their regulations are comparable.[43] Further, the act broadly requires some regulators to coordinate when promulgating rules for a particular regulatory area. For example, under Title VII, SEC and CFTC must coordinate and consult with each other and prudential regulators before starting rulemaking or issuing an order on swaps or swap-related subjects—for the express purpose of assuring regulatory consistency and comparability across the rules or orders. The act also includes specific requirements for CFPB. Title X requires CFPB to consult with the appropriate prudential regulators or other federal agencies, both before proposing a rule and during the comment process, regarding consistency with prudential, market, or systemic objectives administered by such agencies.

Federal financial regulators also have highlighted the importance of coordination during the rulemaking process. For example, in testifying about the need to coordinate agency rulemakings, FSOC's chairperson commented on the importance of coordinating both domestically and internationally to prevent risks from migrating to regulatory gaps—as they did before the 2007-2009 financial crisis—and to reduce U.S. vulnerability to another financial crisis.[44]

At the same time, we noted in a recent report that the FSOC chairperson has recognized the challenges of coordinating on the Dodd-Frank Act rulemakings assigned to specific FSOC members.[45] He noted that the coordination in the rulemaking process represented a challenge because the Dodd-Frank Act left in place a financial system with multiple, independent agencies with overlapping jurisdictions and different responsibilities. However, the chairperson also noted that certain agencies were working much more closely together than they did before the creation of FSOC.

This observation has been repeated by other regulators, whose staffs have told us that interagency coordination in rulemaking has increased since the passage of the Dodd- Frank Act.

Regulators Coordinated as Required, and Such Coordination Involved Around One-Third of Their Dodd-Frank Regulations

We found documentation of coordination among the rulemaking agency and other domestic or international regulators for 19 of the 54 substantive regulations that were issued and became effective between July 21, 2011, and July 23, 2012.

The act required coordination in 16 of the 19 rulemakings. Specifically, 6 of the 19 regulations were jointly issued by two or more regulators and, thus, inherently required interagency coordination (see table 3). The act stipulated coordination for 10 other regulations.

In the Federal Register rule releases, we found evidence documenting the coordination required by the act as well as voluntary coordination with additional regulators. For example, FDIC's regulation on "Certain Orderly Liquidation Authority Provisions" described voluntary coordination with the Federal Reserve.[46]

Similarly, CFTC was required to coordinate with SEC on six swaps regulations it issued, but the agency also coordinated with other regulators on two of those regulations. Further, CFTC coordinated with foreign regulators on all six swaps regulations.

The act did not require coordination for the other three regulations for which we found documentation of coordination, indicating that the agencies voluntarily coordinated. For the remaining 35 regulations that we reviewed, which did not require interagency coordination, we did not find any documentation of coordination among the agencies.[47]

Review of Select Major Rules Highlights Similarities and Differences in Interagency Coordination and the Potential for Related Rules to Differ Despite Coordination

Of the 19 regulations that we identified as having interagency coordination, we selected three regulations to review in depth and sought to cover as many regulators as possible that were required to coordinate under the Dodd-Frank Act (see table 4).

We examined when, how, and the extent to which federal financial regulators coordinated. We also examined efforts undertaken by the regulators to avoid conflicts in the rulemakings.

Table 3. Documentation of Coordination in Releases of Dodd-Frank Regulations, July 21, 2011 through July 23, 2012

Rulemaking	Responsible regulator	Coordination requirement	Nature of coordination	Voluntary coordination[a]
Risk-Based Capital Standards: Advanced Capital Adequacy Framework—Basel II; Establishment of a Risk-Based Capital Floor	FDIC, Federal Reserve, OCC	Yes	Jointly issued rule	Yes[b]
Fair Credit Reporting Risk-Based Pricing Regulations	Federal Reserve, Federal Trade Commission	Yes	Jointly issued rule	N/A
Certain Orderly Liquidation Authority Provisions under Title II of the Dodd-Frank Wall Street Reform and Consumer Protection Act	FDIC	Yes	Act directs FDIC to consult with FSOC. FDIC also consulted with the Federal Reserve.	Yes
Business Affiliate Marketing and Disposal of Consumer Information	CFTC	Yes	Act directs CFTC to consult with numerous other regulators.	N/A
Provisions Common to Registered Entities	CFTC	No	CFTC consulted with prudential regulators	Yes
Debit Card Interchange Fees and Routing	Federal Reserve	Yes	Act directs the Federal Reserve to consult, as appropriate, with numerous other regulators.	N/A
Whistleblower Incentives and Protection	CFTC	No	CFTC consulted with SEC to harmonize the agencies' whistleblower rules.	Yes
Swap Data Repositories: Registration Standards, Duties and Core Principles	CFTC	Yes	Act directs CFTC to coordinate with SEC and other prudential regulators, and foreign regulators as appropriate.	N/A

Table 3. (Continued)

Rulemaking	Responsible regulator	Coordination requirement	Nature of coordination	Voluntary coordination[a]
Resolution Plans Required	FDIC, Federal Reserve	Yes	Jointly issued rule	N/A
Derivatives Clearing Organization General Provisions and Core Principles	CFTC	Yes	Act directs CFTC to coordinate with SEC and other prudential regulators, and foreign regulators as appropriate.	N/A
Real-Time Public Reporting of Swap Transaction Data	CFTC	Yes	Act directs CFTC to coordinate with SEC and other prudential regulators, and foreign regulators as appropriate.	N/A
Swap Data Recordkeeping and Reporting Requirements	CFTC	Yes	Act directs CFTC to coordinate with SEC and other prudential regulators, and foreign regulators as appropriate. CFTC also consulted with the Office of Financial Research (OFR) and the Department of the Treasury.	Yes
Reporting by Investment Advisers to Private Funds and Certain Commodity Pool Operators and Commodity Trading Advisors on Form PF	CFTC, SEC	Yes	Jointly issued rule	N/A
Business Conduct Standards for Swap Dealers and Major Swap Participants With Counterparties	CFTC	Yes	Act directs CFTC to coordinate with SEC and other prudential regulators, and foreign regulators as appropriate. CFTC also consulted with the Department of Labor and Internal Revenue Service.	Yes
Mutual Insurance Holding Company Treated as Insurance Company	FDIC	Yes	Act directs FDIC to consult with FSOC in developing this rule.	N/A

Rulemaking	Responsible regulator	Coordination requirement	Nature of coordination	Voluntary coordination[a]
Swap Dealer and Major Swap Participant Recordkeeping, Reporting, and Duties Rules; Futures Commission Merchant and Introducing Broker Conflicts of Interest Rules; and Chief Compliance Officer Rules for Swap Dealers, Major Swap Participants, and Futures Commission Merchants	CFTC	Yes	Act directs CFTC to coordinate with SEC and other prudential regulators, and foreign regulators as appropriate.	N/A
Alternatives to the Use of External Credit Ratings in the Regulations of the OCC	OCC	No	OCC consulted with FDIC	Yes
Further Definition of "Swap Dealer," "Security-Based Swap Dealer," "Major Swap Participant," "Major Security-Based Swap Participant" and "Eligible Contract Participant"	CFTC, SEC	Yes	Jointly issued rule	N/A
Calculation of Maximum Obligation Limitation	FDIC, Treasury	Yes	Jointly issued rule, in consultation with FSOC	N/A

Source: GAO analysis of the Dodd-Frank Act and the Federal Register.

Note: The rules are ordered by the date that each rule became effective.

[a] Some regulators coordinated with domestic and/or international regulators beyond what was required under the Dodd-Frank Act and, in some cases, where coordination was not required. For rules marked "not applicable" (N/A), the agencies did not coordinate with any agencies beyond what was required.

[b] While section 171 of the Dodd-Frank Act did not mandate that the rule establishing a risk-based capital floor be jointly issued, it did require that the floor be issued on a consolidated basis. To address this provision of the act, the federal banking agencies decided to issue a joint rule

Most Coordination for the Rulemakings Occurred Early in the Process and Was Informal

The regulators held some formal interagency meetings early on in the rulemaking process; however, coordination was mostly informal and conducted through e-mail, telephone conversations, and one-on-one conversations between staff. For example, at the initiation stage of the risk-based capital rulemaking, FDIC, OCC, and the Federal Reserve held a principal-level meeting to discuss the major issues relating to the interpretation of the statutory requirement. After this meeting, staffs formed an interagency working group, comprised of staff from each agency who, according to Federal Reserve staff, continually have worked together on numerous capital rules and therefore have a very close working relationship. Likewise, agency staffs said that after the initial formal meetings on the other rulemakings that we reviewed, coordination revolved around informal staff-level discussions. Coordination during the proposed rule drafting stage typically was characterized by staff-level conversations primarily through telephone calls or e-mails and some face- to-face meetings. Staffs would contact each other as issues arose to work out conflicts or differences in agency viewpoints. When issues could not be resolved at the staff level, they were escalated to senior management, but most issues were resolved and most coordination occurred at the staff level throughout the drafting of the proposed rules, according to agency staffs. For all three rulemakings reviewed, agency staffs coordinated at least weekly through the proposal stage with the frequency of coordination escalating as the proposed rule neared issuance.

After receiving public comments and while preparing the final rule, agency staffs told us that they continued to coordinate with each other, but the need for and level of interagency coordination varied by rule. For instance, OCC, Federal Reserve, and FDIC staffs said that by the time they reached the stage of drafting the final risk-based capital rule, meetings were less frequent because the group already had worked out most of the details. Coordination between CFTC and SEC also decreased during this stage of the real-time reporting rulemaking. Conversely, CFTC and SEC staffs said that interagency coordination continued to be frequent while drafting the final swaps entities rule because after the proposed rule was issued some differences in underlying definitions remained, such as the definition for "highly leveraged." The commissions used public comments to the proposed rule to help them interpret and come to consensus on the definitions. CFTC and SEC staffs met regularly in this period to refine drafts, resolve issues, and convene an industry roundtable.

Table 4. Summary of Three Major Rules Reviewed

Rulemaking	Description of coordination
Risk-Based Capital Standards: Advanced Capital Adequacy Framework—Basel II; Establishment of a Risk-Based Capital Floor	The act requires the appropriate federal banking agencies (i.e., FDIC, OCC and the Federal Reserve) to establish minimum risk-based capital requirements on a consolidated basis for insured depository institutions, depository institution holding companies, and nonbank financial companies supervised by the Federal Reserve.
Further Definition of "Swap Dealer," "Security-Based Swap Dealer," "Major Swap Participant," "Major Security- Based Swap Participant" and "Eligible Contract Participant"	The act directs CFTC and SEC, in consultation with the Federal Reserve, jointly to further define the terms "Swap Dealer," "Security-Based Swap Dealer," "Major Swap Participant," "Major Security- Based Swap Participant," and "Eligible Contract Participant."
Real-Time Public Reporting of Swap Transaction Data	The act directs CFTC to promulgate rules providing for the public availability of swap data in real-time to enhance price discovery. The rule introduces definitions, processes, entities, and other items relevant to the real-time public reporting of swap transaction data.

Source: GAO analysis of information from the Dodd-Frank Act and the Federal Register.

Coordination with International Regulators on the Three Rulemakings Varied

The extent to which agencies coordinated with international regulators varied in the three rulemakings that we reviewed. For example, CFTC and SEC coordinated with international regulators on swap rulemakings. For the real-time reporting rule, CFTC coordinated with foreign regulators, such as the Financial Services Authority and the European Commission, which provided ideas on data reporting. On the swap entities rule, CFTC and SEC staffs said that they participated in numerous conference calls and meetings with various international regulators.

In contrast, the banking regulators did not meet with any international regulators on the risk-based capital rule. The agency staffs said that they were implementing a straightforward statutory provision that required little interpretation and little amendment to the existing rules; therefore, staffs said they did not need to seek input from international regulators as to how to implement U.S. law. Staffs said that for less narrowly scoped rules, where regulators have more discretion, they are more proactive in reaching out to international regulators. FDIC staff cited, as an example, the risk retention rule, for which they reached out to the European Union to understand their approach.[48]

Regulators Worked to Resolve Conflicts but Some Differences Remained

Regulators who were responsible for the three rulemakings that we reviewed said that they tried to identify potential areas of duplication or conflict involving the rules. For the risk-based capital rule, the banking regulators held discussions on regulatory conflict and duplication and concluded that none would be created by this rule. For the swap entity rule and the real-time reporting rule, CFTC and SEC identified potential areas of conflict, which they were able to address through coordination. For example, when developing the real-time reporting rule, CFTC and SEC initially had different approaches about what type of entity would be in charge of disseminating swap transaction data. SEC proposed that only swap data repositories would be required to disseminate real-time data, and CFTC initially proposed to require several different entities to do so.[49] When CFTC issued its final rule, it changed its approach to mirror SEC's proposal, deciding that only swap data repositories would be required to disseminate real-time swap data. Agency staffs said that this harmonization should help to minimize the compliance cost burden placed on market participants and allow for more efficient operation of systems for the public dissemination of swap and security-based swap market data.

In some areas, differences in rules remained after interagency coordination, due to differences in regulatory jurisdiction. In particular, while CFTC and SEC reached consensus on the text for the jointly issued swap entities rule, the regulators outlined different approaches in certain parts of the rule as a result of their regulatory jurisdiction over different product sets. For example, some of the language of the definitions for "major swap participant" and "major security-based swap participant" differs because the agencies each have jurisdiction over different products and some of these products have different histories, markets, and market sizes, according to CFTC and SEC staff. Also, in the real-time reporting rule, CFTC, in its final rule, defined specific data fields to be reported, while SEC, in its proposed rule, outlined broad data categories and required swap data repositories to develop specific reporting protocols. Agency staffs stated that while the approaches were different, they were not inconsistent. The key factors the regulators considered were whether the rules achieved the policy objectives and whether the regulated entities could comply with both agencies' rules given their differences. It was determined that swap data repositories could develop data reporting protocols that would comply with both agencies' rules.

To document and communicate preliminary staff views on certain issues to senior management, regulators use term sheets throughout the rulemaking process. Although term sheets are primarily internal documents, they were shared with staff at other regulators to communicate views and elicit comments. These term sheets serve as a formal mechanism to help initiate discussions of differences in the regulators' positions. Term sheets generally are drafted internally by staff at each agency, shared between or among agency staff, and shared with agency principals or senior management. CFTC and SEC created term sheets for both the swap entities rule and the real-time reporting rule. Conversely, for the risk-based capital rule, the banking regulators did not create a term sheet because, according to OCC staff, the statutory requirements for this rule were explicit and therefore a term sheet was not required. However, staff noted that this was different from a standard rulemaking where they typically would draft and share a term sheet.

Most Agencies Continue to Lack Formal Policies and Procedures to Guide Interagency Coordination

While a few agencies have made progress on developing policies for interagency coordination for their rulemaking, most have not. In November 2011, we reported that most of the federal financial agencies lacked formal policies or procedures to guide their interagency coordination in the rulemaking process.[50] Federal financial regulators informally coordinated on some of the final rules that we reviewed, but most of the agencies lacked written policies and procedures to guide their interagency coordination. Specifically, seven of nine agencies did not have written policies and procedures to facilitate coordination on rulemaking.[51] The written policies and procedures that existed were limited in their scope or applicability. The remaining two regulators, FDIC and OCC, had rulemaking policies that include guidance on developing interagency rules. As we previously reported, documented policies can help ensure that adequate coordination takes place, help to improve interagency relationships, and prevent the duplication of efforts at a time when resources are extremely limited. Since our November 2011 report, we found that OCC and CFPB have further developed guidance on interagency coordination, but the other agencies have not. CFPB has developed guidance that outlines the agency's approach to interagency consultation in rulemaking. The document generally describes two rounds of consultation when drafting the proposed rule and two rounds when addressing comments and drafting the final rule. The guidance highlights the points in a rulemaking at which staff should reach out to other regulators, the purpose of consultation, and the length of time to allow for responses from regulators. Similarly, OCC updated its rulemaking policy to include more detail on what steps should be taken in coordination and who should be involved. In our November 2011 report, we recommended that FSOC work with the federal financial regulators to establish formal coordination policies for rulemaking that clarify issues, such as when coordination should occur, the process that will be used to solicit and address comments, and what role FSOC should play in facilitating coordination. While FSOC has not implemented this recommendation, staff told us that they have developed coordination processes around specific areas of the Dodd-Frank Act. For example, FSOC staff said that they have coordinated closely with FDIC on all rulemakings under Title II. In addition, FSOC developed written guidance for coordination on rulemakings for enhanced prudential standards for bank holding companies with $50 billion or more in total consolidated assets and nonbank financial companies designated by FSOC for Federal Reserve supervision under sections 165 and 166 of the act. However, in a September 2012 report, we noted that a number of industry representatives questioned why FSOC could not play a greater role in coordinating member agencies' rulemaking efforts.[52] In that report, we further noted that the FSOC chairperson, in consultation with the other FSOC members, is responsible for regular consultation with the financial regulatory entities and other appropriate organizations of foreign governments or international organizations. We also reiterated our previous recommendation by stating that FSOC should establish formal collaboration and coordination policies for rulemaking.

Impacts of the Dodd- Frank Act Have Not Yet Fully Materialized and Remain Uncertain

The full impact of the Dodd-Frank Act remains uncertain. Although federal agencies continue to implement the act through rulemakings, much work remains. For example, according to one estimate, regulators have finalized less than half of the total rules that may be needed to implement the act.[53] Furthermore, sufficient time has not elapsed to measure the impact of those rules that are final and effective. As we previously noted, even when the act's reforms are fully implemented, it will take time for the financial services industry to comply with the array of new regulations.[54] The evolving nature of implementation makes isolating the effects of the Dodd-Frank Act on the U.S. financial marketplace difficult. This task is made more difficult by the many factors that can affect the financial marketplace, including factors that could have an even greater impact than the act. Recognizing these limitations and difficulties, we developed a multipronged approach to analyze current data and trends that might be indicative of some of the Dodd-Frank Act's initial impacts, as institutions react to issued and expected rules. First, the act contains provisions that serve to enhance the resilience of certain bank and nonbank financial companies and reduce the potential for financial distress in any one of these companies to affect the financial system and economy. Specifically, the Dodd-Frank Act requires the Federal Reserve to impose enhanced prudential standards and oversight on bank holding companies with $50 billion or more in total consolidated assets and nonbank financial companies designated by FSOC.[55] We developed indicators to monitor changes in certain SIFI characteristics. Although the indicators may be suggestive of the act's impact, our indicators do not identify causal links between their changes and the act. Further, many other factors can affect SIFIs and, thus, the indicators. As new data become available, we expect to update and, as warranted, revise our indicators and create additional ones to cover other provisions. Second, we used difference-in-difference analysis to infer the act's impact on the provision of credit by and the safety and soundness of bank SIFIs. The analysis is subject to limitations, in part because factors other than the act could be affecting these entities. Third, we analyzed the impact of several major rules that were issued pursuant to the Dodd-Frank Act and have been final for around a year or more.

Indicators Suggest Increased SIFI Resiliency and Provide Baselines for Future Analysis

The 2007-2009 financial crisis demonstrated that some financial institutions, including some nonbank financial companies (e.g., AIG), had grown so large, interconnected, complex, and leveraged, that their failure could threaten the stability of the U.S. financial system and the global economy. Financial institutions, markets, and infrastructure that make up the U.S. financial system provide services to the U.S. and global economies, such as helping to allocate funds, allowing households and businesses to manage their risks, and facilitating financial transactions that support economic activity. The sudden collapses and near-collapses of major financial institutions, including major nonbank financial institutions, were among the most destabilizing events of the 2007-2009 financial crisis. In addition, large, complex financial institutions that are perceived to be "too big to fail" can increase uncertainty in periods of market turmoil and reinforce destabilizing reactions within the financial system. According to its legislative history, the Dodd-Frank Act contains provisions intended to reduce the risk of failure of a large, complex financial institution and the damage that such a failure could do to the economy.[56] Such provisions include (1) establishing FSOC to identify and respond to emerging threats to the stability of the U.S. financial system; (2) authorizing FSOC to designate a nonbank financial company for Federal Reserve supervision if FSOC determines it could pose a threat to the financial stability of the United States based on the company's size, leverage, interconnectedness, or other factors; and (3) directing the Federal Reserve to impose enhanced prudential standards and oversight on bank holding companies with $50 billion or more in total consolidated assets (referred to as bank SIFIs in this report) and nonbank financial companies designated by FSOC (referred to as nonbank SIFIs in this report). The Dodd-Frank Act also is intended to reduce market expectations of future federal rescues of large, interconnected, and complex firms using taxpayer dollars.[57] Under the act, bank holding companies with $50 billion or more in total consolidated assets and nonbank financial companies designated by FSOC for Federal Reserve supervision are required to develop plans for their rapid and orderly resolution. Additionally, FDIC is given new orderly liquidation authority to act as a receiver of a troubled financial firm whose failure could threaten financial stability so as to protect the U.S. financial system and the wider economy.

Some Dodd-Frank Act provisions may result in adjustments to SIFIs' size, interconnectedness, complexity, leverage, or liquidity over time.[58] We developed indicators to monitor changes in some of these SIFI characteristics.[59] The size and complexity indicators reflect the potential for a single company's financial distress to affect the financial system and economy. The leverage and liquidity indicators reflect a SIFI's resilience to shocks or its vulnerability to financial distress. FSOC has not yet designated any nonbank financial firms for Federal Reserve supervision.[60] As a result, we focus our analysis on U.S. bank SIFIs.[61] Our indicators have limitations. For example, the indicators do not identify causal links between changes in SIFI characteristics and the act. Rather, the indicators track or begin to track changes in the size, complexity, leverage, and liquidity of SIFIs over the period since the Dodd-Frank Act was passed to examine whether the changes are consistent with the act. However, other factors—including the economic downturn, international banking standards agreed upon by the Basel Committee on Banking Supervision (Basel Committee), European debt crisis, and monetary policy actions—also affect bank holding companies and, thus, the indicators.[62] These factors may have a greater effect than the Dodd-Frank Act on SIFIs. In addition, some rules implementing SIFI-related provisions have not yet been proposed or finalized. Thus, trends in our indicators include the effects of these rules only insofar as SIFIs have changed their behavior in response to issued rules and in anticipation of expected rules. In this sense, our indicators provide a baseline against which to compare future trends.

Table 5 summarizes the changes in our bank SIFI indicators. The size indicators do not provide a clear trend between the third quarter of 2010 and the second quarter of 2012. Additionally, we have only one data point in the complexity indicator, but our data suggest that the largest bank SIFIs generally were more complex organizationally than other bank SIFIs. Lastly, the indicators suggest that bank SIFIs, on average, have become less leveraged since the third quarter of 2010, and their liquidity also appears to have improved. Trends in our leverage and liquidity indicators appear to be consistent with an improvement in SIFIs' resilience to shocks.

Table 5. Summary of Trends in Indicators for U.S. Bank SIFIs, from Third Quarter 2010 through Second Quarter 2012

Characteristic	Indicator (italicized) and description of trend	Consistent with decreased, no change, or increased spillover effects or resilience?
Size – Size captures the amount of financial services or financial intermediation that a bank holding company provides.	*The number of large bank SIFIs* remained the same, and the *number of other bank SIFIs* decreased slightly.[a] Median *assets for large bank SIFIs* and median *assets for other bank SIFIs* increased slightly.[a, b] The median *market share (measured in assets) for bank SIFIs* remained relatively constant.[b]	Consistent with no change in spillover effects

Table 5. (Continued)

Characteristic	Indicator (italicized) and description of trend	Consistent with decreased, no change, or increased spillover effects or resilience?
Interconnectedness – Interconnectedness captures direct or indirect linkages between financial institutions that may transmit distress from one institution to another.	None[c]	N/A
Complexity – Operational complexity may reflect an institution's diverse lines of business and locations in which the institution operates.	The *number of legal entities of large bank SIFIs* was large relative to other bank SIFIs as of October 2012.[a] Almost all large bank SIFIs have a high *number or percentage of legal entities located outside of the United States*, and the *number of countries where the foreign entities are located* is also high.	N/A
Leverage– Leverage can be defined broadly as the ratio between some measure of risk exposure and capital that can be used to absorb unexpected losses from the exposure. Traditionally, it has referred to the use of debt, instead of equity, to fund an asset and been measured by the ratio of total assets to equity on the balance sheet.	The median *tangible common equity as a percent of total assets for bank SIFIs* increased slightly.[b] The median *tangible common equity as a percent of risk-weighted assets for bank SIFIs* increased slightly.[b]	Consistent with increasedresilience
Liquidity– Liquidity represents the ability of an institution to fund its assets and meet its obligations as they become due.	The median *short-term liabilities as a percent of total liabilities for bank SIFIs* decreased.[b] The median *liquid assets as a percent of short-term liabilities for bank SIFIs* increased.[b]	Consistent with increased resilience

Sources: GAO analysis of SNL Financial data and Federal Reserve Board data from the National Information Center.

[a] Large bank SIFIs are those with $500 billion or more in assets. Other bank SIFIs are those with assets between $50 billion and $500 billion.

[b] To calculate the median measures, we calculated the relevant indicator measure for each bank holding company, and then reported the median for large bank SIFIs, the median for other bank SIFIs, the median for non-SIFI banks, or the median for the entire group.

[c] We plan to develop indicators for interconnectedness in future reports.

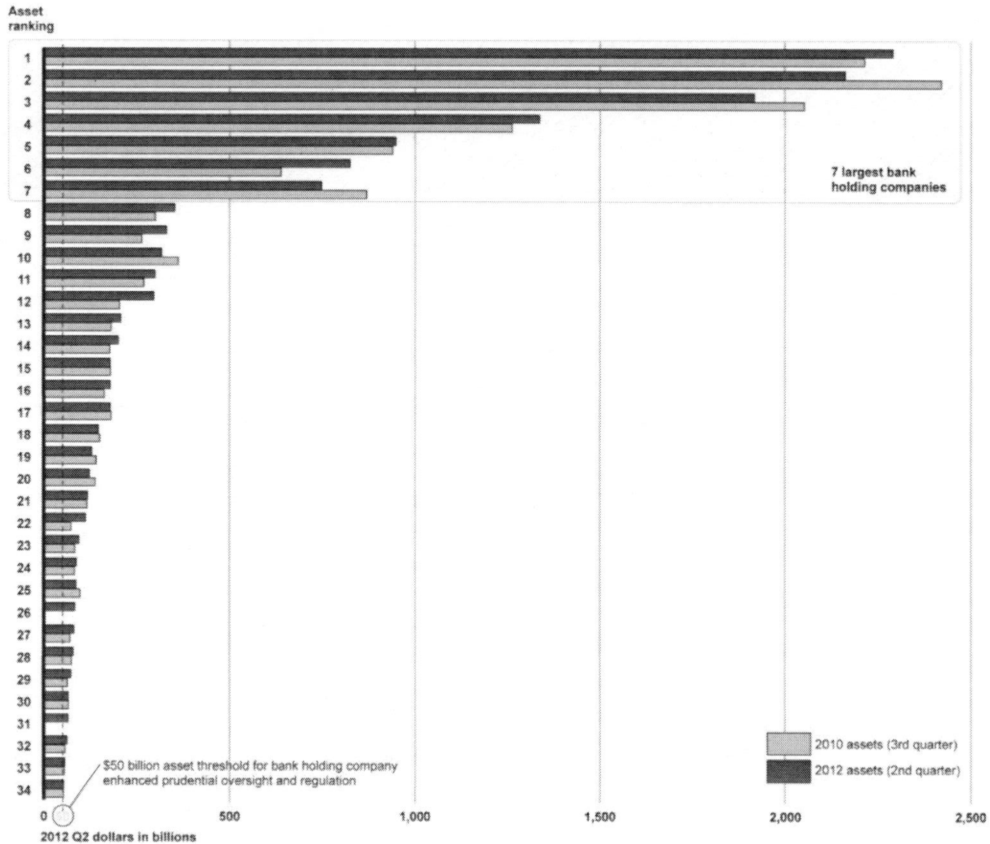

Source: GAO analysis of SNL Financial and Bureau of Economic Analysis data.

Note: Bank SIFIs are U.S. bank holding companies with $50 billion or more in total consolidated assets. Bank SIFIs are ranked by assets as of the second quarter of 2012, with 1 being the bank SIFI with the most assets and 34 being the bank SIFI with the least assets. The figure shows assets for these bank SIFIs as of the third quarter of 2010 and the second quarter of 2012 adjusted for inflation and measured in billions of constant 2012 Q2 dollars.

Figure 1. Total Assets of U.S. Bank SIFIs, as of the Third Quarter of 2010 and Second Quarter of 2012.

Table 6. Number and Median Size of U.S. Bank Holding Companies and U.S. Bank SIFIs, at the End of Calendar Year Unless Otherwise Noted (Assets in Billions of 2012 Q2 Dollars)

		2010	2011	2012 Q2
Total bank holding companies	Number	1,006	1,014	1,028
	Median assets	$1.0	$0.9	$0.9
Total SIFIs	Number	36	34	34
	Median assets	$155.7	$177.3	$162.6
Large SIFIs	Number	7	7	7
	Median assets	$1,294.3	$1,325.5	$1,336.2
Other SIFIs	Number	29	27	27
	Median assets	$114.2	$128.2	$117.5
Non-SIFIs	Number	970	980	994
	Median assets	$0.9	$0.9	$0.9

Source: GAO analysis of SNL Financial data.

Note: Median assets are adjusted for inflation and are measured in billions of constant 2012 Q2 dollars. We define large bank SIFIs are those with assets of $500 billion or more. Other bank SIFIs are those with assets between $50 billion and $500 billion. Non-SIFI bank holding companies are those with assets less than $50 billion but greater than $500 million.

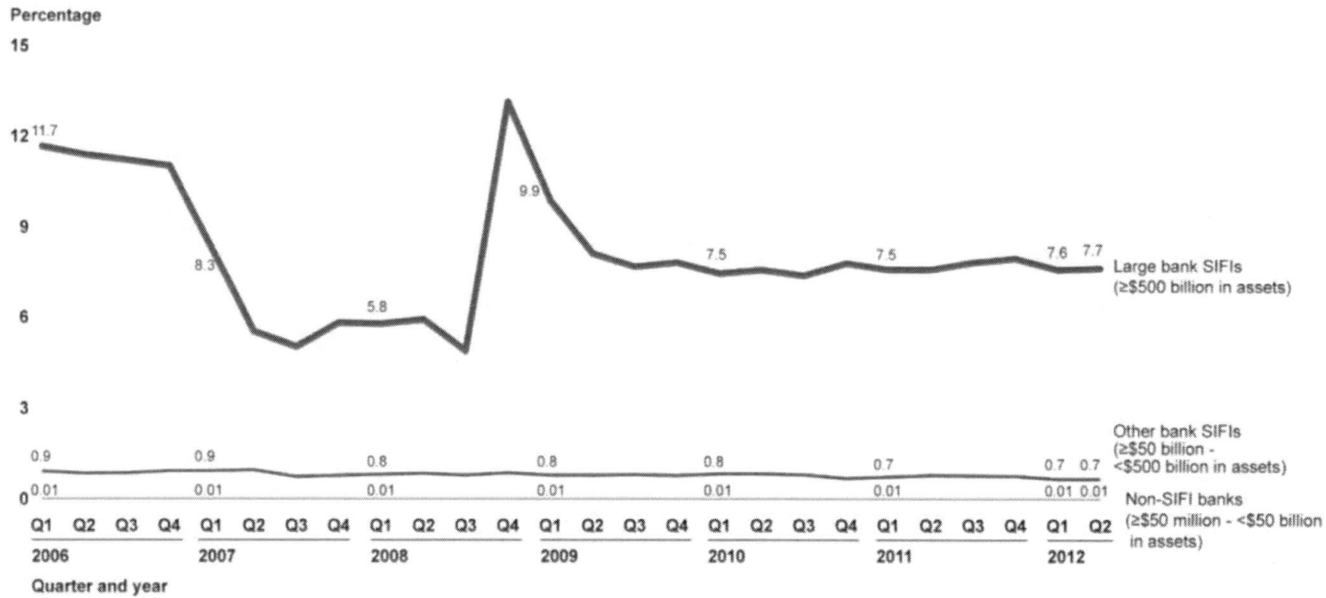

Source: GAO analysis of SNL Financial data.

Note: To calculate the median market shares, we calculated the market share for each bank holding company, and then reported the median market share for large bank SIFIs, the median for other bank SIFIs, and the median for non-SIFI banks.

Figure 2. Median Market Share for U.S. Bank Holding Companies by Size, from First Quarter of 2006 through Second Quarter of 2012.

SIFI Size

The three size indicators generally did not show a clear change in the size of U.S. bank SIFIs between 2010 and 2012. In 2009, the Federal Reserve chairman noted that regulators have strong incentives in a crisis to prevent the failure of a large, highly interconnected financial firm because of the risks such a failure would pose to the financial system and the broader economy.[63] He also noted that market participants' belief that a particular firm is considered too big to fail has many undesirable effects, such as reducing market discipline and providing an artificial incentive for firms to grow to be perceived as too big to fail. The Dodd-Frank Act contains provisions that may discourage or inhibit large financial institutions (including those we refer to as SIFIs) from increasing their size. For example, the act's $50 billion-asset threshold for determining which bank holding companies are subject to enhanced regulation by the Federal Reserve may discourage certain institutions from increasing or encourage others to reduce their assets to avoid such regulation. Also, some provisions and related rules allow or require regulators to limit, in certain circumstances, the size of a SIFI by imposing restrictions on its growth, activities, or operations. Although implicit or explicit limits on the size of a financial institution may prevent the institution from growing so large that it is perceived by the market as too big to fail, such limits also may prevent the institution from achieving economies of scale and benefiting from diversification.[64]

We developed three indicators of size. The first indicator tracks the number of bank SIFIs. The second indicator measures a SIFI's size based on the total assets on its balance sheet. The third indicator measures the extent to which industry assets are concentrated among the individual SIFIs, reflecting a SIFI's size relative to the size of the industry. A limitation of these indicators is that they do not include an institution's off-balance sheet activities and thus may understate the amount of financial services or intermediation an institution provides. Furthermore, asset size alone is not an accurate determinant of systemic risk, as an institution's systemic risk significance also depends on other factors, such as its complexity and interconnectedness.

As shown in figure 1, seven U.S. bank SIFIs had more than $500 billion in total consolidated assets (referred to as large bank SIFIs in this report) in the third quarter of 2010 and in the second quarter of 2012.[65] The large bank SIFIs were considerably larger than the other bank SIFIs.

The three indicators show that the number and size of U.S. bank SIFIs have remained largely the same over the past 2 years and that several SIFIs dominate the market.

- Table 6 shows that the total number of large U.S. bank SIFIs has remained at 7 and the total number of other bank SIFIs decreased from 29 to 27 between 2010 and the second quarter of 2012. Over the same period, the median assets for large bank SIFIs and other bank SIFIs increased slightly.
- Figure 2 shows that the median market share for large bank SIFIs was about 7.7 percent of the industry's total assets at the end of the second quarter of 2012, roughly the same market share as in the third quarter of 2010. The median market share for other bank SIFIs hovered between 0.7 percent and 0.8 percent of the industry's total assets during that time frame.

Complexity of SIFIs

Our complexity measure indicates that large U.S. bank SIFIs are likely relatively more complex than other U.S. bank SIFIs. Interconnectedness and complexity of operations or organizational structure are related concepts. Interconnectedness refers to linkages among financial companies that may transmit distress from one company to another. Operational complexity, which reflects a company's diverse lines of business and locations of operation, may make interconnected firms harder to resolve in case they fail. According to FSOC, in the years preceding the crisis, the structure of many financial institutions had become complex and interconnections among financial institutions were poorly understood. The belief that highly interconnected and complex companies were more likely to receive government support during a financial crisis promoted moral hazard problems for such institutions.[66]

Some Dodd-Frank Act provisions may result in increased transparency regarding the interconnectedness and complexity of SIFIs or in reductions in their interconnections and complexity. For example, Title II provides FDIC with new authority to resolve nonviable financial firms that pose a significant threat to U.S. financial stability. Moreover, section 165 of the act requires bank holding companies with $50 billion or more in total consolidated assets and nonbank financial companies designated by FSOC for Federal Reserve supervision to submit to regulators periodic resolution plans that describe a company's strategy for rapid and orderly resolution in the event of material stress or failure.[67] FSOC has recommended that firms use the development of the plans as an opportunity to reduce organizational complexity, and some regulators and experts have noted that the development of the resolution plans may lead some SIFIs to simplify their operations.[68] Our indicators of complexity are the number of legal entities of bank SIFIs, the percentage of foreign legal entities of large SIFIs, and the number of countries where they are located. An institution's operational complexity may reflect an institution's diverse lines of business and locations in which the institution operates, which are reflected partly through its various legal structures. Consequently, a SIFI with a large number of legal entities—particularly foreign ones operating in different countries under different regulatory regimes—may be more difficult to resolve than a SIFI with fewer legal entities in fewer countries. One limitation of our indicator is that it does not provide information on the relative complexity of SIFIs resulting directly from their various lines of business. Additionally, changes in the operational complexity of a SIFI may be reflected in our indicators only insofar as they result in a change in the number of legal entities.

The complexity indicators show that large U.S. bank SIFIs have a relatively large number of legal entities compared with other U.S. bank SIFIs and that they operate in various countries, suggesting that they may be more complex.

- Figure 3 shows that 6 of 7 large bank SIFIs had more than 2,300 legal entities, with two of them having almost 7,000 and 11,000. The median number of legal entities for large SIFIs was 4,160, while the median for the remaining 27 bank SIFIs was 109. Within this group, the maximum number of legal entities for a bank holding company was 787, but 21 of the 27 bank holding companies had less than 200 legal entities.
- Table 7 shows that almost all large U.S. bank SIFIs have a high number or percentage of legal entities located outside of the United States and that these legal entities operate in numerous different countries. For example, bank SIFI 3, 5, and 7 all have thousands of foreign legal entities operating in 81, 60, and 55 different countries, respectively.

Unlike size, leverage, or liquidity measures, interconnectedness measures are a relatively new concept, and academics are developing ways to capture the various types of interconnectedness that may lead to financial instability.[69] For this report, we did not develop indicators for interconnectedness but expect to do so in the future. The Financial Stability Board (FSB), with the help of the Basel Committee, has designated eight U.S bank holding companies, including the largest seven bank SIFIs, as globally systemically important banks (G-SIB), largely based on its assessment of the companies' interconnectedness and complexity.[70] The Basel Committee's G-SIB designation process uses a variety of quantitative indicators to rate each global bank holding company on its size, interconnectedness, global cross-jurisdictional activity, complexity, and availability of substitutes or financial institution infrastructures for the services produced. As we work to develop interconnectedness indicators, we will monitor the status of the G-SIB designation process.[71]

SIFI Leverage

Our leverage indicators show that U.S. bank SIFIs have decreased their leverage between 2010 and the second quarter of 2012, which may suggest that the average U.S. bank SIFI, all else equal, has become more resilient to shocks since 2010. Leverage generally refers to the use of debt, instead of equity, to fund an asset, but can be defined more broadly as the ratio between some measure of risk exposure and capital that can be used to absorb unexpected losses from the exposure. According to federal regulators, the recent financial crisis exposed significant weaknesses in the regulatory capital requirements for large banking companies. Specifically, the amount and quality of capital held by many large, complex banking companies during the crisis proved inadequate to cover the companies' risks. To address weaknesses in capital requirements, federal banking regulators are implementing reforms under the Dodd-Frank Act and the Basel Committee that require better capitalization; that is, less leverage and higher quality capital.[72] These reforms may cause SIFIs to reduce their leverage.[73] For example, as part of its proposed enhanced prudential standards for bank holding companies with $50 billion or more in total consolidated assets and nonbank financial companies designated by FSOC, the Federal Reserve would require all of these companies to submit annual capital plans, conduct stress tests, and hold sufficient capital to better ensure that the firms can survive during periods of stress.[74] In addition, the Federal Reserve plans to propose a risk-based capital surcharge on at least some SIFIs that is based on the capital surcharge for G-SIBs.[75] Although there are many ways to measure leverage, we use two measures: (1) tangible common equity as a percent of total assets, and (2) tangible common equity as a percent of risk-weighted assets.[76] The two indicators differ, in part because total risk-weighted assets reflect some of an institution's off-balance sheet activity but total assets do not.

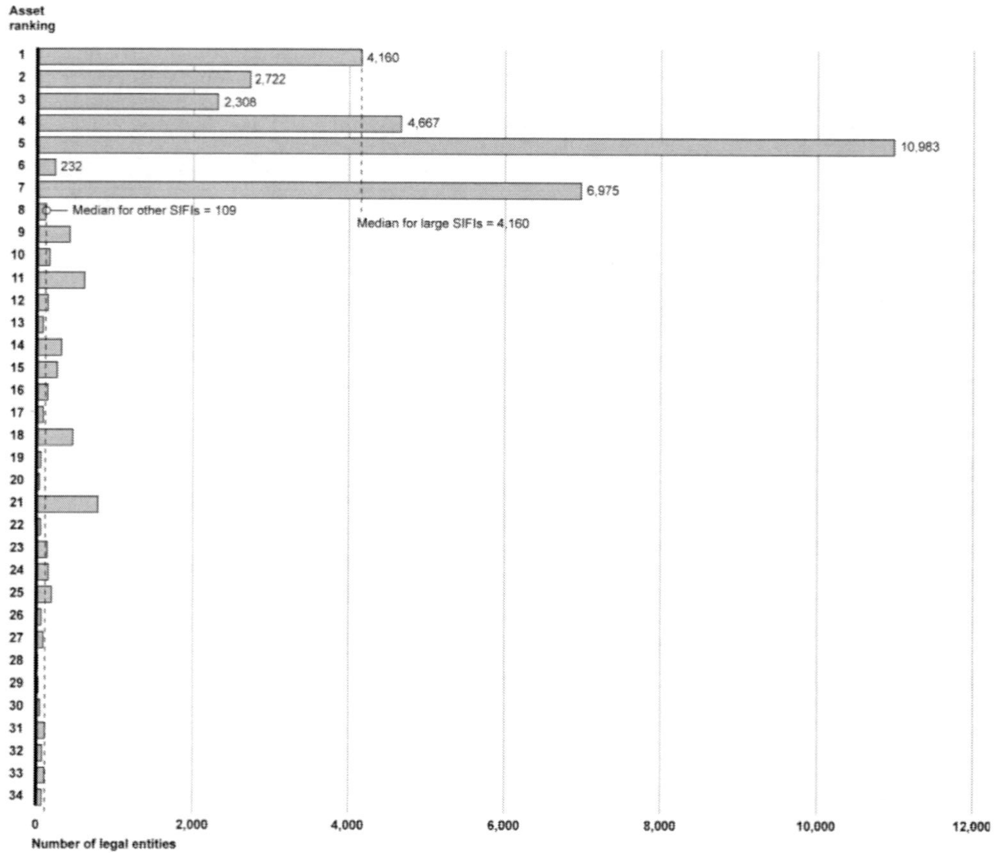

Source: GAO analysis of federal Reserve Board data from the National Information Center.

Note: Bank SIFIs are ranked by assets as of the second quarter of 2012, with 1 being the bank SIFI with the most assets and 34 being the bank SIFI with the least assets.

Figure 3. Total Legal Entities of U.S. Bank SIFIs, as of October 23, 2012.

Table 7. Foreign Legal Entities of Large U.S. Bank SIFIs, as of October 22, 2012

Bank SIFI ranking	Total number of legal entities	Number and percent of foreign legal entities	Number of countries where foreign entities are located
Bank SIFI 1	4,144	777 (19%)	51
Bank SIFI 2	2,559	656 (26%)	47
Bank SIFI 3	2,308	1,239 (54%)	81
Bank SIFI 4	4,666	227 (5%)	27
Bank SIFI 5	10,974	5,697 (52%)	60
Bank SIFI 6	232	188 (81%)	37
Bank SIFI 7	7,039	3,927 (56%)	55

Source: GAO analysis of National Information Center data maintained by the Federal Reserve.

Note: Large bank SIFIs are those with assets of $500 billion or more. Bank SIFIs are ranked by assets as of the second quarter of 2012, with 1 being the bank SIFI with the most assets.

We focus on tangible common equity, because it most closely approximates the amount of capital available to absorb losses in asset values in the short term. A limitation of both indicators is that they may not fully reflect an institution's exposure to risk. Total assets do not reflect an institution's risk exposure from off-balance sheet activities and generally treat all assets as equally risky.

The calculation of risk-weighted assets is designed to reflect differences in risk, but the weights assigned to the assets may not fully reflect the risk exposure associated with those assets, for example, because assets in broad categories of loans all receive the same risk weight.

Both indicators show that U.S. bank SIFIs are less leveraged:

- Figure 4 shows that SIFIs' median tangible common equity as a percent of total assets has increased from the third quarter of 2010 to the second quarter of 2012, continuing an upward trend since the beginning of 2009.
- Figure 5 shows that SIFIs' median tangible common equity as a percent of risk-weighted assets, which include off-balance sheet activity, has also increased from the third quarter of 2010 to the second quarter of 2012, continuing an upward trend since the middle of 2009.

SIFI Liquidity

Our indicators suggest that U.S. bank SIFIs have improved their liquidity, which may indicate that they, on average, have become more resilient to shocks since 2010.

Liquidity represents the ability of a financial institution to fund its assets and meet its obligations as they become due.

Liquidity risk is the risk of not being able to obtain funds at a reasonable price within a reasonable time period to meet obligations as they become due. According to Federal Reserve staff, the 2007-2009 financial crisis illustrated that under strained market conditions, sources of liquidity can quickly disappear, and firms may be unable to meet their obligations, potentially leading to insolvency.

As with capital and leverage requirements, the Dodd-Frank Act and Basel III contain reforms that address liquidity risk and may result in improvements in the liquidity of SIFIs.[77]

For example, as part of the enhanced prudential standards for bank holding companies with $50 billion or more in total consolidated assets and nonbank financial companies designated by FSOC for Federal Reserve supervision, the Federal Reserve has proposed imposing liquidity risk management standards that require company-run liquidity stress tests and a contingency funding plan.[78]

The proposed regulations also require a liquidity buffer to meet projected cash outflows. In addition, the Federal Reserve plans to propose liquidity requirements on at least some SIFIs based on Basel III's liquidity requirements, as implemented in the United States.[79]

We developed two indicators to analyze changes in SIFI liquidity: (1) short-term liabilities as a percent of total liabilities and (2) liquid assets as a percent of short-term liabilities.[80]

Short-term liabilities are balance sheet obligations due within 1 year; an institution's short-term liabilities as a percent of total liabilities are a measure of its need for liquidity.

Liquid assets can easily be sold without affecting their price and, thus, can be easily converted to cash to cover debts that come due. Accordingly, liquid assets as a percent of an institution's short-term liabilities are a measure of access to liquidity.

For example, if this percentage is under 100 percent, the institution does not have sufficient access to liquidity and is unlikely to have enough liquid assets to cover its short-term debt. A limitation of both of these indicators is that they do not include off-balance sheet liabilities, such as callable derivatives or potential derivatives- related obligations.

The second indicator also does not include off- balance sheet liquid assets, such as short-term income from derivative contracts.[81]

Both liquidity indicators suggest that U.S. bank SIFIs have improved their liquidity since the third quarter of 2010. The figures also show that large bank SIFIs held relatively more short-term liabilities but also relatively more liquid assets to cover such liabilities than other bank SIFIs.

- Figure 6 shows that median short-term liabilities as a percent of total liabilities declined from the third quarter of 2010 through the second quarter of 2012 for both large and other SIFIs.
- Figure 7 shows that median short-term (or liquid) assets as a percent of short-term liabilities increased for both large and other SIFIs during the same period.

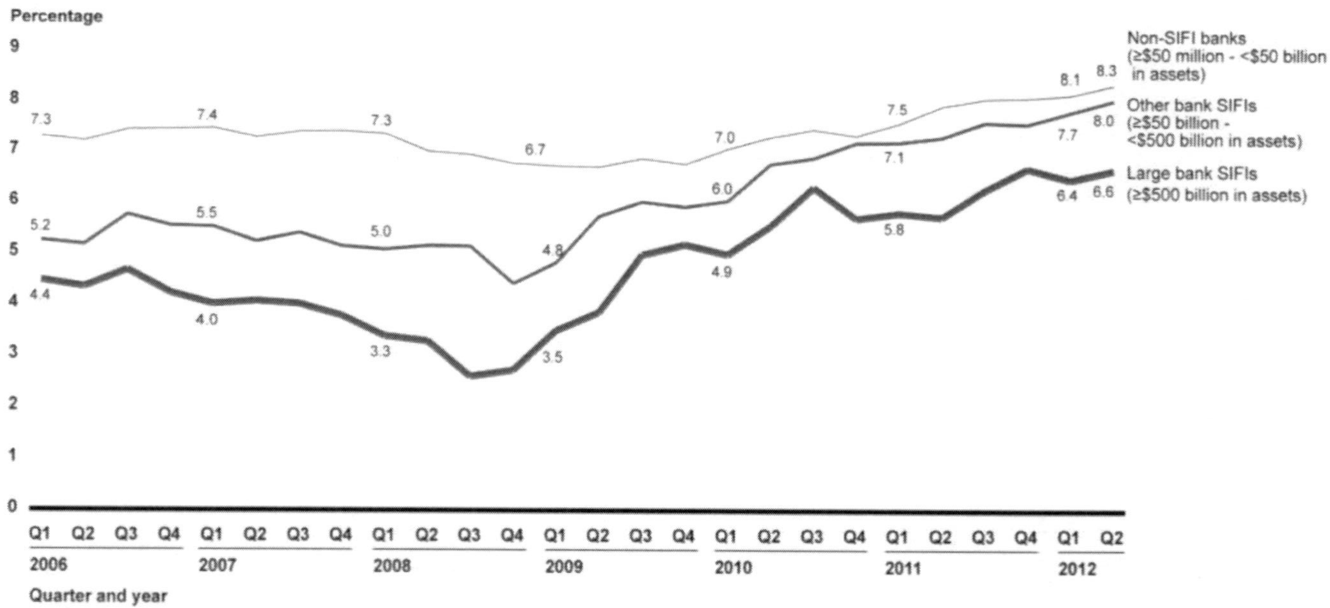

Source: GAO analysis of SNL Financial data.

Note: To calculate median tangible common equity as a percent of assets, we calculated this percentage for each bank holding company, and then reported the median for large bank SIFIs, the median for other bank SIFIs, and the median for non-SIFI banks.

Figure 4. Median Tangible Common Equity as a Percent of Total Assets for U.S. Bank Holding Companies by Size, from First Quarter of 2006 through Second Quarter of 2012.

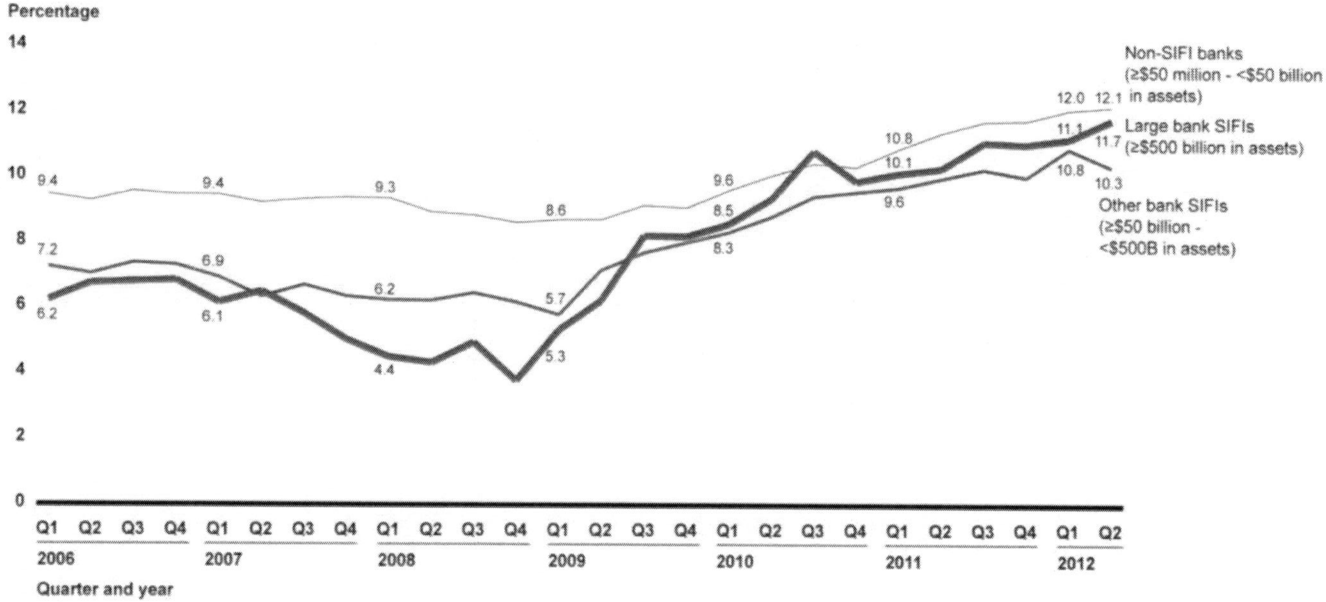

Source: GAO analysis of SNL Financial data.

Note: To calculate median tangible common equity as a percent of risk-weighted assets, we calculated this percentage for each bank holding company, and then reported the median for large bank SIFIs, the median for other bank SIFIs, and the median for non-SIFI banks.

Figure 5. Median Tangible Common Equity as a Percent of Risk-Weighted Assets for U.S. Bank Holding Companies by Size, from First Quarter of 2006 through Second Quarter of 2012.

New Requirements for Bank SIFIs Initially Appear to Have Affected Minimally the Cost of SIFI-Provided Credit and Enhanced SIFIs' Safety and Soundness

According to our regression analysis, the Dodd-Frank Act has been associated with minimal increases in the cost of credit provided by U.S. bank SIFIs and an increase in the safety and soundness of the SIFIs.[82] As we have noted, the Dodd-Frank Act requires the Federal Reserve to impose a variety of regulatory reforms on SIFIs, including enhanced risk- based capital, leverage, and liquidity requirements. These reforms may affect not only the safety and soundness of bank SIFIs but also the cost and availability of credit provided by bank SIFIs. Although capital and leverage requirements may help reduce the probability of a firm failing and promote financial stability, they could cause firms to raise lending rates and also limit firms' ability to provide credit, especially during a crisis. Similarly, while stricter liquidity requirements may help reduce the probability of a firm failing and promote financial stability, companies could respond to these requirements by increasing lending spreads to offset lower yields on assets or longer maturities on liabilities. To the extent that they increase the cost and reduce the availability of credit, these reforms may lead to reduced output and economic growth.[83]

As mentioned earlier, the Dodd-Frank Act subjects some bank holding companies to enhanced oversight and regulation but not other bank holding companies. Specifically, the act requires the Federal Reserve to impose a number of enhanced prudential standards on bank holding companies with total consolidated assets of $50 billion or more. These prudential standards must include enhanced risk-based capital and leverage requirements, enhanced liquidity requirements, enhanced risk- management and risk committee requirements, single-counterparty credit limits, stress tests, and a debt-to-equity limit for bank holding companies that FSOC has determined pose a grave threat to the stability of the financial system if the imposition of such a limit is necessary to mitigate the risk.[84] The Federal Reserve published proposed rules to implement these requirements on January 5, 2012.[85] Under the proposed rules, bank holding companies with $50 billion or more in total consolidated assets would be subject to the enhanced prudential standards beginning on the first day of the fifth quarter following the effective date of a final rule. On the other hand, bank holding companies with less than $50 billion in total consolidated assets are not subject to the Board's enhanced prudential standards.

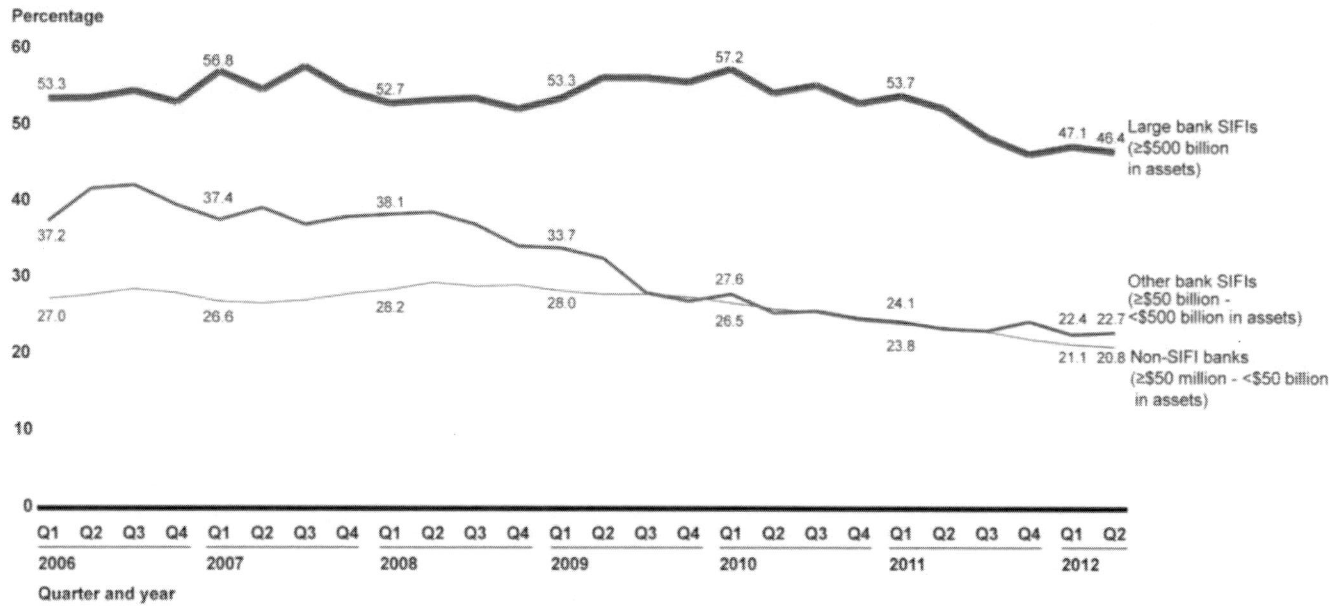

Source: GAO analysis of SNL Financial data.

Note: To calculate median short-term liabilities as a percent of total liabilities, we calculated this percentage for each bank holding company, and then reported the median for large bank SIFIs, the median for other bank SIFIs, and the median for non-SIFI banks.

Figure 6. Median Short-Term Liabilities as a Percent of Total Liabilities for U.S. Bank Holding Companies by Size, from First Quarter of 2006 through Second Quarter of 2012.

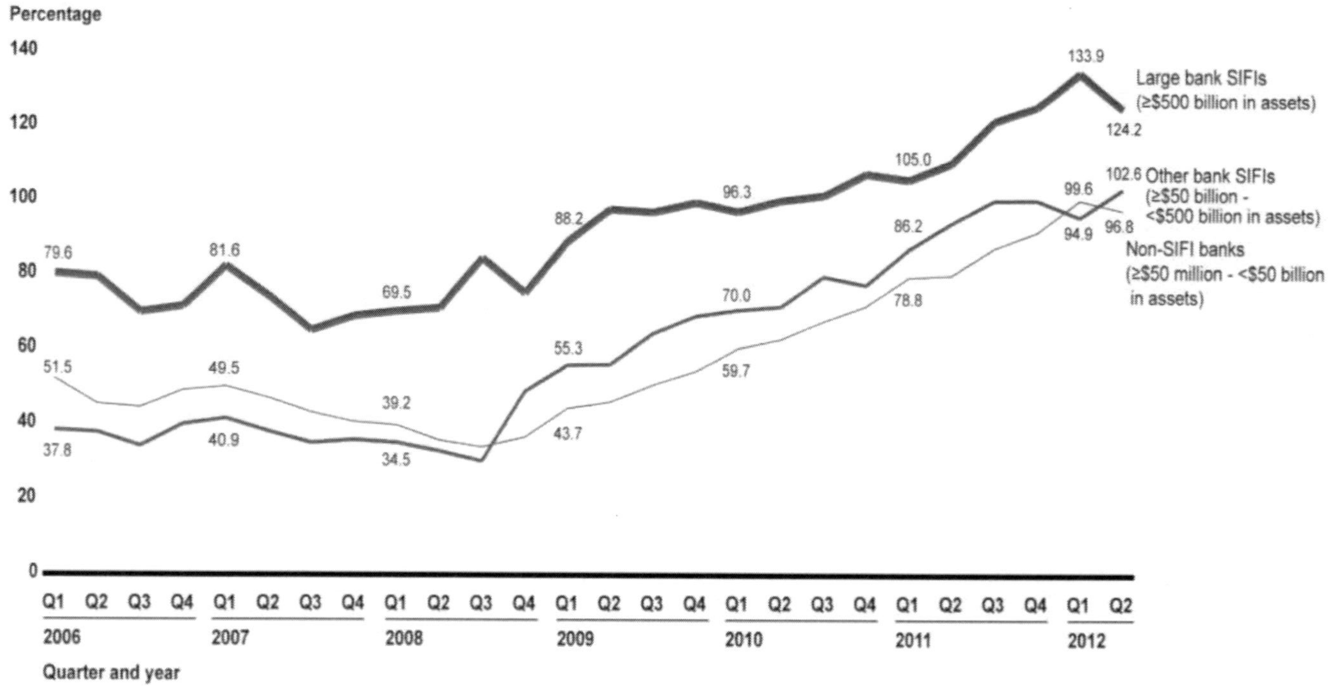

Source: GAO analysis of SNL Financial data.

Note: To calculate median liquid assets as a percent of short-term liabilities, we calculated this percentage for each bank holding company, and then reported the median for large bank SIFIs, the median for other bank SIFIs, and the median for non-SIFI banks.

Figure 7. Median Liquid Assets as a Percent of Short-term Liabilities for U.S. Bank Holding Companies by Size, from First Quarter of 2006 through Second Quarter of 2012.

Table 8. Estimated Changes in U.S. Bank SIFIs' Funding Cost and Measures of Safety and Soundness Associated with the Dodd-Frank Act, from Third Quarter 2010 through Second Quarter 2012

Variable	Measured as	Range of statistically significant estimated changes (percentage points)	Quarters estimated changes are statistically significant
Cost of credit indicator			
Funding cost	Interest expense as a percent of interest-bearing liabilities	0.05	2012 Q2
Safety and soundness indicators			
Capital adequacy	Tangible common equity as a percent of total assets	1.16 to 1.66	2010 Q3-2012 Q2
	Tangible common equity as a percent of risk-weighted assets	1.70 to 2.24	2010 Q3-2012 Q2
Asset quality	Performing assets as a percent of total assets	1.04 to 1.32	2010 Q3-2012 Q2
Earnings	Earnings as a percent of total assets	0.10 to 0.24	2010 Q3-2011 Q3
Liquidity	Liquid assets as a percent of volatile liabilities	No statistically significant estimated changes	None
	Stable liabilities as a percent of total liabilities	2.82 to 5.67	2010 Q3-2012 Q2

Source: GAO analysis of data from the Federal Reserve and SNL Financial.

Notes: We analyzed data for bank holding companies from the first quarter of 2006 through the second quarter of 2012. We estimated the effects of the new SIFI requirements on bank SIFIs by regressing the variables listed in the table on indicators for each bank holding company, indicators for each quarter, indicators for whether a bank holding company is a SIFI for each quarter from the third in 2010 through the second in 2012, and other variables controlling for size, foreign exposure, securitization income, other nontraditional income, and participation in the Troubled Asset Relief Program. Estimated changes are the coefficients on the indicators for whether a bank holding company is a SIFI in each quarter from the third in 2010 through the second in 2012. We used t-tests to assess whether the coefficient on the SIFI indicator for a specific quarter was significant at the 5 percent level. For more information on our methodology, see appendix IV.

As a result, we can compare funding costs, capital adequacy, asset quality, earnings, and liquidity for bank SIFIs and non-SIFI bank holding companies before and after the implementation of the enhanced prudential requirements. All else being equal, the difference in the comparative differences is the inferred effect of the Dodd-Frank Act on bank SIFIs. While many of the SIFI-related rulemakings have yet to be implemented, our estimates are suggestive of the initial effects of the Dodd-Frank Act on bank SIFIs and provide a baseline against which to compare future results.[86]

Our estimates suggest that the Dodd-Frank Act is associated with an increase in U.S. bank SIFIs' funding costs in the second quarter of 2012, but it is not associated with either an increase or decrease in other quarters (table 8). From the third quarter of 2010 to the second quarter of 2012, bank SIFIs' funding cost ranged from about 0.02 percentage points lower to about 0.05 percentage points higher than it otherwise would have been since the Dodd-Frank Act was enacted. However, the estimates are not individually statistically significant for quarters other than the second quarter of 2012. These estimates suggest that the act's new requirements for SIFIs have had little effect on U.S. bank SIFIs' funding costs, at least until recently. To the extent that the cost of credit provided by bank SIFIs is a function of their funding costs, the new requirements for SIFIs are likely to have had little effect on the cost of credit to date.

Table 8 also shows that the Dodd-Frank Act is associated with improvements in most measures of U.S. bank SIFIs' safety and soundness. Bank SIFIs appear to be holding more capital than they otherwise would have held in every quarter since the Dodd-Frank Act was enacted. The quality of assets on the balance sheets of bank SIFIs also seems to have improved since the Dodd-Frank Act was enacted. The act is associated with higher earnings for bank SIFIs in the first four quarters after the act's enactment. It is also associated with improved liquidity as measured by the extent to which a bank holding company is using stable sources of funding. The only measure that has not clearly improved since the act's enactment was liquidity as measured by the capacity of a bank holding company's liquid assets to cover its volatile liabilities. Thus, the Dodd-Frank Act appears to be broadly associated with improvements in most indicators of safety and soundness for U.S. bank SIFIs.

Our approach allows us to partially differentiate changes in funding costs, capital adequacy, asset quality, earnings, and liquidity associated with the Dodd-Frank Act from changes due to other factors. However, several factors make isolating and measuring the impact of the Dodd-Frank Act's new requirements for SIFIs challenging. The effects of the act cannot be differentiated from the effects of simultaneous changes in economic conditions, such as the pace of the recovery from the recent recession, or regulations, such as those stemming from Basel III, or other changes, such as in credit ratings that differentially may affect bank SIFIs and other bank holding companies. In addition, many of the new requirements for SIFIs have yet to be implemented. For example, the Federal Reserve plans to impose a capital surcharge and liquidity ratios on at least some SIFIs, but the exact form and scope of these requirements are not yet known.[87] Nevertheless, our estimates are suggestive of the initial effects of the Dodd-Frank Act on bank SIFIs and provide a baseline against which to compare future trends.

Analysis of Select Major Rules Identifies Some Initial Impacts, but the Markets Have Not Yet Fully Adjusted to the Rules

We analyzed the impact of four major rules that were issued separately by the Federal Reserve and SEC pursuant to the Dodd-Frank Act and have been final for around a year or more.[88] In contrast to the Dodd-Frank Act's SIFI-related provisions and rules, these major rules implement provisions that serve specific investor or consumer protection purposes. These impact analyses are limited in scope and preliminary in nature, in part, because of the limited time the rules have been effective and limited data available on their impact. In addition, as discussed below, financial and other firms subject to the rules and other market participants still are reacting to the rules.

We reviewed the following four major rules: (1) the Federal Reserve's Regulation II (Debit Card Interchange Fees and Routing), (2) SEC's Issuer Review of Assets in Offerings of Asset-Backed Securities rule, (3) SEC's Disclosure for Asset-Backed Securities Required by Section 943 of the Dodd-Frank Wall Street Reform and Consumer Protection Act rule, and (4) SEC's Shareholder Approval of Executive Compensation and Golden Parachute Compensation rules. We selected these rules because they were major rules and some data were available about their impact.[89] Appendix V includes a more complete discussion of our impact analysis on the Federal Reserve's Regulation II.

The Federal Reserve's Regulation II (Debit Interchange Fees and Routing Rule)

Section 1075 of the Dodd-Frank Act amends the Electronic Fund Transfer Act (EFTA) by adding a new section 920 on interchange transaction fees and rules for payment card transactions. As required by EFTA section 920, the Federal Reserve's Regulation II establishes standards for assessing whether debit card interchange fees received by issuers are reasonable and proportional to the costs incurred by issuers for electronic debit transactions. The rule sets a cap on the maximum permissible interchange fee that an issuer may receive for an electronic debit transaction at $0.21 per transaction, plus 5 basis points multiplied by the transaction's value.[90] An issuer bank that complies with Regulation II's fraud-prevention standards may receive no more than an additional 1 cent per transaction.[91] The fee cap became effective on October 1, 2011. However, as required by EFTA section 920, the rule exempts from the fee cap issuers that have, together with their affiliates, less than $10 billion in assets, and transactions made using debit cards issued pursuant to government-administered payment programs or certain reloadable prepaid cards.

Regulation II's fee cap generally has reduced debit card interchange fees.[92] However, debit card issuers, payment card networks, and merchants are continuing to react to the rule; thus, the rule's impact has not yet been fully realized. Large banks that issue debit cards initially have experienced a decline in their debit interchange fees as a result of the rule, but small banks generally have not.[93] Data published by the Federal Reserve show that 15 of 16 card networks provided a lower interchange fee, on average, to issuers subject to the fee cap (covered issuers) after the rule took effect.[94] Specifically, the data show that the average interchange fee received by covered issuers declined 52 percent, from $0.50 in the first three quarters of 2011 to $0.24 in the fourth quarter. During the same period, the interchange fee as a percentage of the average transaction value for covered issuers declined from 1.29 percent to 0.60 percent. Our regression analysis also suggests that the fee cap is associated with reduced interchange fee income for covered banks.[95] Our estimates suggest that interchange fees collected by covered banks, as a percent of their assets, were about 0.007 to 0.008 percentage points lower than they otherwise would have been in the absence of the fee cap. For a bank with assets of $50 billion, this amounts to $3.5 million to $4 million in reduced interchange fee income per quarter.[96]

The reduction in debit interchange fees following the adoption of Regulation II likely has resulted or will result in savings for merchants. According to the Federal Reserve and industry experts, the merchant acquirer market is competitive. Thus, the decrease in interchange fees likely has translated or will translate into lower merchant acquirer fees.[97] However, merchants that have a high volume of small value transactions may be worse off after the adoption of the rule, because their debit card interchange fees might have increased due to the fee cap.[98]

In addition to the fee cap, Regulation II prohibits issuers and card networks from restricting the number of networks over which electronic debit transactions may be processed to less than two unaffiliated networks.[99] This prohibition became effective on April 1, 2012. The rule further prohibits issuers and networks from inhibiting a merchant from directing the routing of an electronic debit transaction over any network allowed by the issuer.[100] This prohibition became effective October 1, 2011.

Regulation II's prohibitions may have a limited impact on increasing competition and, in turn, lowering interchange fees, because issuers largely control which networks may process their debit card transactions. Merchants likely continue to have only one network routing option for transactions completed by signature.[101]

Additionally, issuers can comply by having an unaffiliated signature network and personal identification number (PIN) network, which means that there may only be one network routing choice once the customer decides to use her signature or her PIN. Therefore, even though Regulation II provides merchants with the authority to choose the network over which to route debit card transactions, merchants may not have a choice about which network to route a debit card transaction.

Going forward, issuers may be able to act strategically to limit competition over debit card interchange fees through their control over which networks may process their debit card transactions.

In response to Regulation II, VISA is undertaking strategies intended to attract merchant routing. VISA recently imposed a new monthly fixed acquirer fee that merchants must pay to accept VISA debit and credit cards. VISA also plans to reduce merchants' variable fees so that merchants' total fees associated with VISA transactions likely would be lower after the new fee structure's implementation.[102] In addition, according to VISA representatives, VISA's signature network also is able to process PIN transactions, in essence automatically offering an additional PIN routing choice to merchants for cards that carry VISA signature.[103] For example, in the past, a debit card that carried the VISA signature and two other PIN networks usually would process a PIN transaction through one of the PIN networks. Now, the VISA check card signature network can continue to be the only option for routing signature debit transactions on that card but also become a third option for routing PIN debit transactions. The extent to which such strategies may lower debit card interchange fees is unknown.

SEC's Rules on Asset-Backed Securities Disclosures and Reviews

Section 945 of the Dodd-Frank Act requires SEC to issue a rule relating to the registration statement required to be filed by issuers of asset- backed securities (ABS). To implement section 945, SEC adopted a new rule under the Securities Act of 1933 and amending Regulation AB.[104] The rule requires an issuer of registered offerings of ABS to perform a review of the assets underlying the securities that "must be designed and effected to provide reasonable assurance that the disclosure in the prospectus regarding the assets is accurate in all material respects."[105] The rule requires disclosure regarding: "[t]he nature of the review of assets conducted by an ABS issuer;" "[t]he findings and conclusions of a review of assets conducted by an ABS issuer or third party;" "[d]isclosure regarding assets in the pool that do not meet the underwriting standards;" and "[d]isclosure regarding which entity determined that the assets should be included in the pool . . . ."[106] This rule became effective on March 28, 2011.

Section 943 of the Dodd-Frank Act requires SEC to prescribe regulations on the use of representations and warranties in the market for ABS. The new rules promulgated under section 943 require ABS securitizers to disclose fulfilled and unfulfilled repurchase requests.[107] Specifically, ABS securitizers must disclose demand, repurchase, and replacement history for an initial 3-year look back period ending December 31, 2011, and going forward on a quarterly basis. Further, the rules conform disclosure requirements for prospectuses and ongoing reports for ABS sold in registered transactions. The rule also requires nationally recognized statistical rating organizations to disclose in any report accompanying a credit rating for an ABS transaction, the representations, warranties, and enforcement mechanisms available to investors and how they differ from the representations, warranties and enforcement mechanisms in issuances of similar securities. This rule became effective on March 28, 2011.

The two SEC ABS rules may increase issuer securitization costs but also investor demand by improving investor confidence in the market for ABS. The effect of the rules on the revitalization of the ABS markets is unclear. Isolating and estimating the effects of the SEC rules on the ABS market is challenging, but data on ABS issuances are available. However, factors other than the SEC rules likely impact ABS issuance trends much more significantly. For example, the ABS markets compete with other capital markets for investor dollars, so yields or potential returns to investments in competing markets may be an important determinant of ABS activity. Additionally, ABS are backed by residential mortgage, commercial mortgage, equipment, student, auto, credit card, and other loans, which means that the health of those underlying markets also may determine the extent to which financial institutions may be able and willing to securitize the loans and investors may be willing to invest in ABS.

Since 2010, ABS issuances of agency mortgage-related assets declined slightly but appear to be stabilizing, while total issuances for other types of ABS continue to be at historically low levels. Figure 8 shows that ABS issuances in total historically have been dominated by agency mortgage-related ABS. At the height of market issuances in 2003, agency mortgage-related ABS made up about 76 percent (or $3.4 trillion) of the almost $4.5 trillion dollars in total issuances, and between 2008 and 2011, they comprised about 91 percent of annual ABS issuances.[108] Agency mortgage-related ABS issuances declined to 2004 levels in 2011, but the data for the first two quarters of 2012 indicate that this recent downward trend may be stabilizing.

Figure 9 shows that issuances of other U.S. ABS have not rebounded from the sharp declines experienced after 2006.[109] From 2006 to 2008, annual issuances of other U.S. ABS (i.e. total U.S. ABS excluding agency mortgage-related ABS) fell by approximately 90 percent from over $1.8 trillion to less than $187 billion, due primarily to 59 and 32 percent drops in non-agency mortgage-related and home equity ABS issuances, respectively.[110] Between 2008 and 2010, issuances of other ABS continued to decline slightly to just over $147 billion.

As shown in figure 9's insert, other ABS issuances have experienced modest increases since 2010, primarily because of the growth in credit card, auto, and student loans ABS.

SEC's Rules on Shareholder Approval of Executive Compensation and Golden Parachute Compensation Arrangements

Section 951 of the Dodd-Frank Act amends the Securities Exchange Act of 1934, requiring public companies subject to the proxy rules to conduct a separate shareholder advisory vote on compensation for executives at least every 3 years and a shareholder advisory vote on the frequency of these votes at least every 6 years.

The amendment also requires a shareholder advisory vote on whether to approve certain so-called "golden parachute" compensation arrangements in connection with a business merger or acquisition transaction.[111]

The rule promulgated under section 951 requires a separate shareholder vote on compensation of executives and a vote on the frequency of these votes for the first annual or other meeting of shareholders at which directors will be elected and for which SEC's rules require executive compensation disclosure pursuant to item 402 of Regulation 5-K occurring on or after January 21, 2011.[112] The rule became effective on April 4, 2011. However, SEC adopted a temporary exemption for smaller reporting companies that does not require them to conduct shareholder advisory votes on executive compensation and their frequency until after January 21, 2013.[113]

Two proxy seasons have passed since SEC's say-on-pay rule became effective for larger reporting firms, and most companies have received majority shareholder approval of their executive compensation packages.[114] Table 9 shows historical data on companies' proposals on executive compensation subject to shareholder vote (say-on-pay proposals).[115] The data show that nearly 3,200 companies provided shareholders with say-on-pay proposals in 2011.

In that year, 2,809 Russell 3000 companies had say-on-pay proposals and around 99 percent of the proposals were approved.[116] A study by the Council of Institutional Investors found that the most frequently cited reason for shareholder opposition for failed proposals conducted between January 1 and July 1, 2011, was a disconnect between pay and performance.[117] Table 9 also shows that in 2012 (as of June 25, 2012), 1,842 companies in the index had say-on-pay proposals and around 97 percent of the proposals were approved.[118] According to SEC, around 1,200 smaller reporting companies are required to hold say-on-pay proposals in 2013. In addition, according to the Institutional Shareholder Services (ISS), a large proxy advisory firm, investors overwhelmingly have supported that future say-on-pay votes be done annually.[119]

Although it is not clear how companies will react to the results of shareholder say-on-pay votes in the future, according to two experts, some failed votes have led to, among other actions, shareholder lawsuits and changes in pay practices. For example, according to the law firm Davis Polk & Wardwell LLP corporate governance blog, as of September 5, 2012, shareholders at a number of public companies that had failed votes have brought lawsuits against the boards of directors, but the courts largely have ruled in favor of the public companies. In its study, Semler Brossy also found that 26 out of 30 companies that had failed say-on-pay proposals in 2011 had passed their 2012 proposals (as of September 2012) due, in part, to changes in pay practices.[120] Additionally, the study noted that companies that received modest shareholder approval of say-on-pay proposals in 2011 also have improved their records. According to the study, 93 of 125 companies that received from 50 percent to 70 percent shareholder approval of say-on-pay proposals in 2011 received more support in 2012.

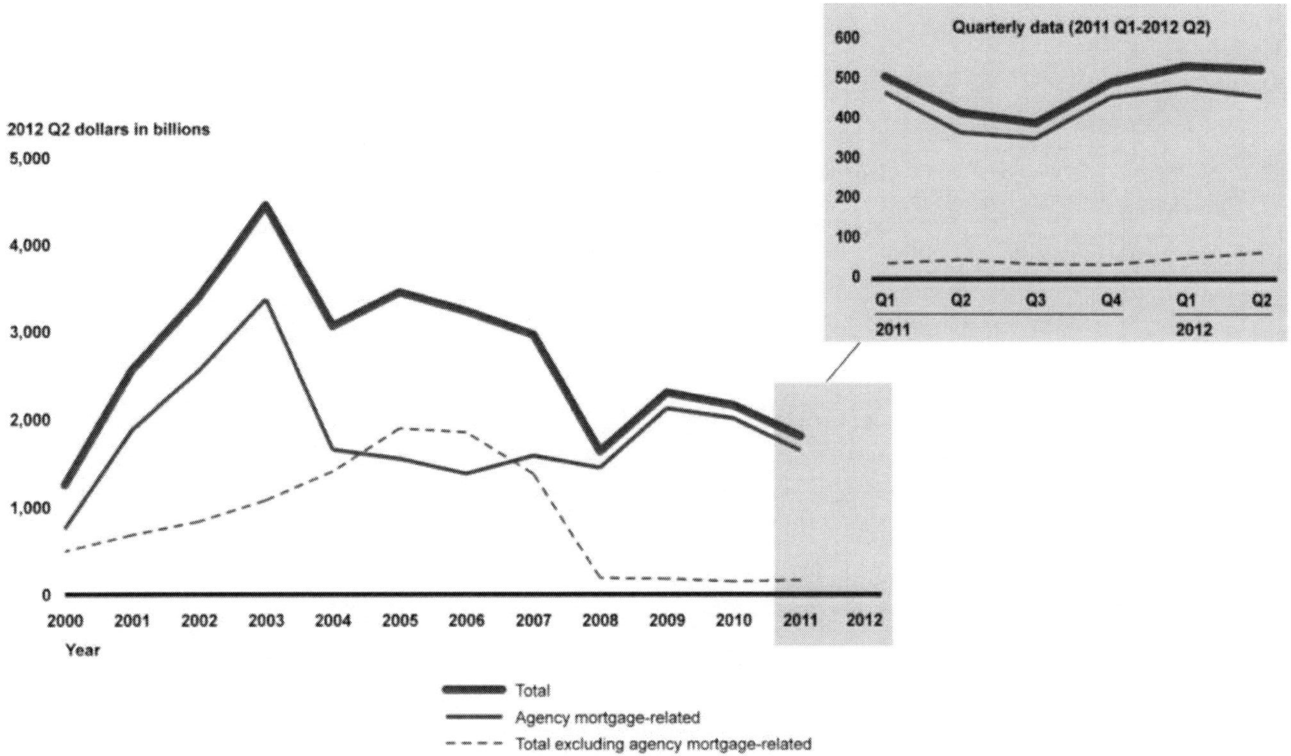

Source: Securities Industry and Financial Markets Association.

Note: Dollar amounts are adjusted for inflation and are expressed in billions of 2012 Q2 dollars.

Figure 8. Annual and Quarterly U.S. ABS Issuance, from 2000 through Second Quarter of 2012.

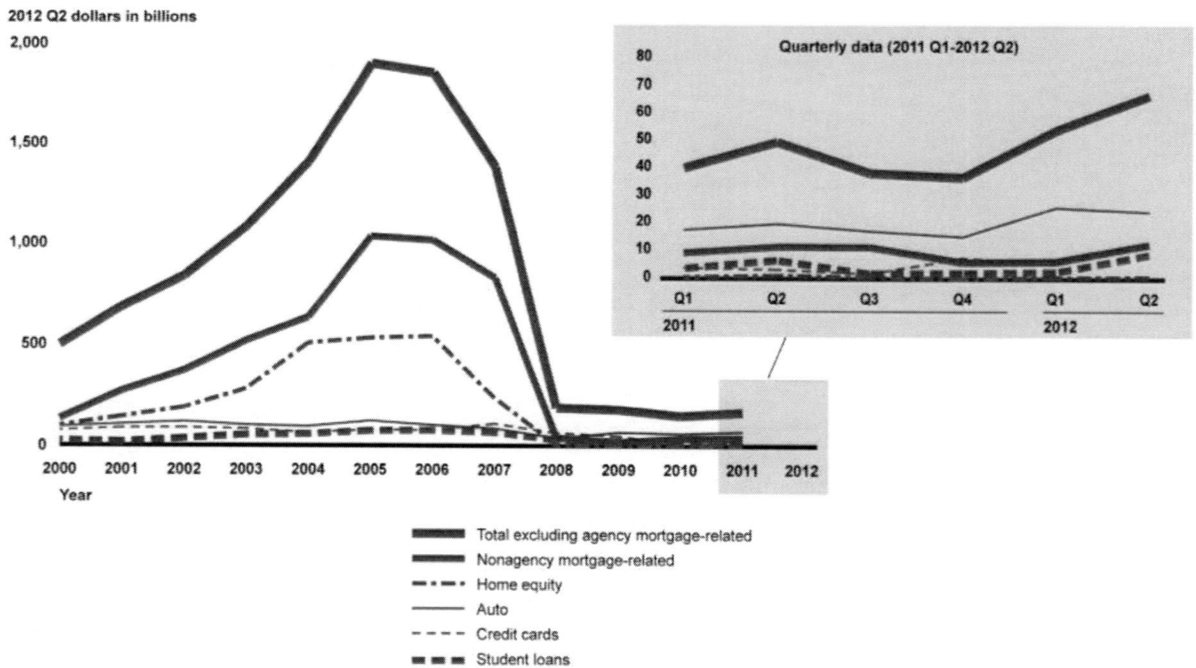

Source: Securities Industry and Financial Markets Association.

Note: Figure 9 does not include agency mortgage-related ABS data. Data on equipment, manufactured housing, and other ABS are not separately plotted but are included in the total. Dollar amounts are adjusted for inflation and are expressed in billions of 2012 Q2 dollars.

Figure 9. Annual and Quarterly U.S. ABS Issuance Excluding Agency Mortgage-Related ABS, from 2000 through Second Quarter of 2012.

Table 9. Public Companies' Say-on-Pay Proposals, from 2007 through June 25, 2012

Year	U.S. Total	Russell 3000 Companies	
	Say-on-pay proposals	Say-on-pay proposals	Failed say-on-pay proposals(percent failed)[a]
2007	6	2	0 (0%)
2008	13	8	0 (0%)
2009	331	154	0 (0%)
2010	326	154	3 (2%)
2011	3,188	2,809	41 (1%)
Jan. 1, 2012- June 25, 2012[b]	2,203	1,842	49 (3%)

Source: GAO summary of data from Institutional Shareholder Services, Inc.

[a] A shareholder can choose to vote "for" or "against" a say-on-pay proposal. She can also choose to take a neutral stance and submit an "abstain" vote. If a shareholder fails to provide instructions to her broker, the corresponding votes are categorized as "broker non-votes." ISS defined failed proposals as those where the "against" votes outnumber the "for" votes.

[b] ISS data for 2012 include say-on-pay proposals as of June 25, 2012, which likely capture most of the 2012 proposals, because votes usually take place between March and June.

Note: Companies that held say-on-pay votes on executive compensation proposals before 2011 include companies that have received financial assistance under the Troubled Asset Relief Program (TARP). These companies have been required to hold annual say-on-pay votes until they pay back all the money they borrowed from the government, at which time they will become subject to the say-on- pay rules applicable to other public companies.

AGENCY COMMENTS AND OUR EVALUATION

We provided a draft of this report to CFPB, CFTC, FDIC, the Federal Reserve Board, FSOC, NCUA, OCC, OFR, SEC, and Treasury for review and comment.

SEC and Treasury provided written comments. All of the agencies also provided technical comments, which we have incorporated, as appropriate.

In their comments, the agencies neither agreed nor disagreed with the report's findings. In its letter, Treasury noted that FSOC agrees that successful implementation of the Dodd-Frank Act rulemakings will require member agencies to work together, even if such coordination is not specifically required under the Dodd-Frank Act.

Treasury also noted that FSOC has served as a forum for discussion among members and member agencies, through various FSOC meetings, committee meetings, and subcommittee meetings. Finally, the letter describes FSOC's effort to continue monitor potential risks to the financial stability and implement other statutory requirements.

In its letter, SEC noted that it revised its guidance on economic analysis in March 2012, in part in response to a recommendation in our 2011 report that federal financial regulators more fully incorporate OMB's regulatory analysis guidance into their rulemaking policies.

SEC's letter stated that the revised guidance already has improved the quality of economic analysis in its rulemakings and internal rule-writing processes.

SEC also noted that FSOC has fostered a healthy and positive sense of collaboration among the financial regulators.

SEC remains amenable to working with FSOC on formal coordination policies, as GAO previously recommended, but noted that FSOC's efforts should fully respect the independence of the respective member agencies regarding the substance of the rules for which they are responsible and the mission of FSOC itself.

A. Nicole Clowers
Director
Financial Markets and
Community Investment

Appendix I. Scope and Methodology

Our objectives in this report were to examine (1) the regulatory analyses, including benefit-cost analyses, federal financial regulators have performed to assess the potential impact of selected final rules issued pursuant to the Dodd-Frank Act; (2) how federal financial regulators consulted with each other in implementing selected final rules issued pursuant to the Dodd-Frank Act to avoid duplication or conflicts; and (3) what is known about the impact of the final Dodd-Frank Act regulations on the financial markets.

To address the first two objectives, we limited our analysis to the final rules issued pursuant to the Dodd-Frank Act that were effective between July 21, 2011, and July 23, 2012, a total of 66 rules (see app. II).

To identify these rules, we used a website maintained by the Federal Reserve Bank of St. Louis that tracks Dodd-Frank Act regulations. We corroborated the data with information on Dodd-Frank Act rulemaking compiled by the law firm Davis Polk & Wardwell LLP.

To address our first objective, we reviewed statutes, regulations, GAO studies, and other documentation to identify the benefit-cost or similar analyses federal financial regulators are required to conduct in conjunction with rulemaking.

For each of the 66 rules within our scope, we prepared individual summaries using a data collection instrument (DCI). The criteria used in the DCI were generally developed based on the regulatory analyses required of federal financial regulators and Office of Management and Budget (OMB) Circular A-4, which is considered best practice for regulatory analysis. We used the completed summaries to develop a table showing the extent to which the federal financial regulators addressed the criteria for each of the Dodd-Frank Act regulations.

We selected 4 of the 66 rules for in-depth review, comparing the benefit-cost or similar analyses to specific principles in OMB Circular A-4. We selected the rules for in-depth review based on whether the rule was deemed a major rule (i.e., whether it is anticipated to have an annual effect on the economy of $100 million or more) by the responsible agency and OMB. We generally found that the financial regulators do not state in the Federal Register notice whether the rule is major.

However, we learned that regulators are required to submit major rules to GAO under the Congressional Review Act (CRA) for the purpose of ensuring that the regulators followed certain requirements in conducting the rulemaking, and GAO maintains a database of major rules.

Our search of the CRA database showed that federal financial regulators issued 19 major Dodd- Frank Act rules within our scope. To further narrow the list of rules for in- depth review, we determined to include at least one rule from each of the federal financial regulators.

We identified major rules issued by only three financial regulators: the Commodity Futures Trading Commission (CFTC), the Board of Governors of the Federal Reserve (Federal Reserve), and the Securities and Exchange Commission (SEC). In addition, the Department of the Treasury (Treasury) issued a major rule during the scope period.

The Federal Reserve and Treasury each issued only one major rule during our scope period—the Debit Card Interchange Fee rule and the Assessment of Fees on Large Bank Holding Companies to Cover the Expenses of the Financial Research Fund, respectively. SEC and CFTC issued multiple major rules during the period.

To further narrow the list of rules for in-depth review, we determined to include only rules implementing a new regulatory authority rather than amending a preexisting regulatory authority. For SEC, only one rule met this criterion—the Securities Whistleblower Incentives and Protections rule. CFTC issued several major rules that met this criterion so to further narrow the list of rules for in-depth review, we consulted with a former CFTC economist and solicited his opinion whether it would be appropriate for GAO to assess the Real-Time Public Reporting of Swap Transaction Data rule, and he agreed.

To compare these rules to the principles in Circular A-4, we developed a DCI with the principles and applied the DCI to all four rules. In conducting each individual analysis, we reviewed the *Federal Register* notices prepared by the agencies during the course of the rulemaking. We also interviewed officials from CFTC, the Federal Reserve, SEC, and Treasury to determine the extent to which benefit-cost or similar analyses were conducted.

To address our second objective, we reviewed the Dodd-Frank Act, regulations, and studies, including GAO reports, to identify the coordination and consultation requirements federal financial regulators are required to conduct in conjunction with rulemaking.

For each of the 66 rules in our scope, we reviewed the rule releases to determine the rules on which agencies coordinated with other federal financial regulators and international financial regulators.

From our review of the rule releases, we developed a table that shows the rules that involved coordination, agencies involved, nature of coordination, whether coordination was required or voluntary, and whether the agencies coordinated with international regulators.

Rules that may have involved interagency coordination in the rulemaking but did not expressly mention such coordination in the rule release are not included in this table. Of the 19 rules that we determined involved interagency coordination, we selected 3 rules to review in depth to assess how and the extent to which federal financial regulators coordinated, focusing on actions they took to avoid conflict and duplication in rulemakings.

In selecting rules to review in depth, we sought to include at least one rule that was jointly issued and therefore implicitly required coordination and at least one rule that was issued by a single agency and involved coordination with another agency. We also sought broad coverage of agencies issuing substantive Dodd- Frank Act rules. We ultimately selected two joint rules and one rule issued by a single agency, including rules issued by FDIC, OCC, Federal Reserve, CFTC, and SEC.

In reviewing each rule, we reviewed the *Federal Register* notices for each rule, and we interviewed officials from each agency to determine how and the extent to which coordination took place to avoid duplication and conflict. We also interviewed officials at FSOC and CFPB to get an understanding of their role in interagency coordination for Dodd-Frank Act rulemakings.

To address our third objective, we took a multipronged approach to analyze what is known about the impact of the Dodd-Frank Act on the financial marketplace. First, the act contains provisions that serve to enhance the resilience of certain bank and nonbank financial companies and reduce the potential for any one of these companies to affect the financial system and economy.

Specifically, the Dodd-Frank Act requires the Federal Reserve to impose enhanced prudential standards and oversight on bank holding companies with $50 billion or more in total consolidated assets and nonbank financial companies designated by FSOC.

For purposes of this report, we refer to these bank and nonbank financial companies as bank systemically important financial institutions (bank SIFI) and nonbank systemically important financial institutions (nonbank SIFI), respectively, or collectively as SIFIs. We developed indicators to monitor changes in certain characteristics of SIFIs that may be suggestive of the impact of these reforms.

FSOC has not yet designated any nonbank financial firms for Federal Reserve enhanced supervision.

As a result, we focus our analysis on U.S. bank SIFIs.[121] To understand the rationale behind the act's focus on enhanced SIFI regulation and oversight, we reviewed the legislative history of the act, the act itself, related regulations, academic studies, GAO and agency reports, and other relevant documentation. To inform our choice of indicators, we analyzed the provisions and related rulemakings most relevant to bank SIFIs.

Our analysis and indicators for this report focus on bank SIFIs' asset size, interconnectedness, complexity, leverage, and liquidity. We developed our indicators of bank SIFIs' size, leverage, and liquidity using quarterly data for bank holding companies from SNL Financial and quarterly data on the gross domestic product (GDP) deflator from the Bureau of Economic Analysis, both for the period from 2006 quarter 1 to 2012 quarter 2.[122]

We developed our indicators of bank SIFIs' complexity using data from the Federal Reserve Board's National Information Center as of October 2012.[123] As new data become available, we expect to update and, as warranted, revise our indicators and create additional indicators to cover other provisions.[124]

Second, we use difference-in-difference regression analysis to infer the act's impact on the provision of credit by and the safety and soundness of U.S. bank SIFIs.

The key element of our analysis is that the Dodd-Frank Act subjects some bank holding companies to enhanced oversight and regulation but not other bank holding companies. Specifically, the act requires the Federal Reserve to impose a number of enhanced prudential standards on bank holding companies with total consolidated assets of $50 billion or more (bank SIFI), while bank holding companies with assets less than $50 billion (non-SIFI banks) are not subject to such enhanced oversight and regulation.

As a result, we were able to compare funding costs, capital adequacy, asset quality, earnings, and liquidity for bank SIFIs and non-SIFI banks before and after the Dodd-Frank Act. All else being equal, the difference in the differences is the inferred effect of the Dodd-Frank Act on bank SIFIs. For our analysis, we used quarterly data on bank holding companies from SNL Financial and quarterly data on commercial banks and savings banks from FDIC and the Federal Financial Institutions Examinations Council, all for the period from 2006 quarter 1 to 2012 quarter 2 (see app. IV for details). Lastly, for all of our indicators, we obtained and addressed high-level comments and suggestions from FSOC staff and two other market experts.

Third, we analyze the impact of several major rules that were issued pursuant to the Dodd-Frank Act and have been final for around a year or more. There were 44 final rules as of July 21, 2011, 7 of which were major rules. We judgmentally selected 4 out of those 7 rules for impact analyses, based largely on data availability.

Our selected rules implement provisions that serve specific investor or consumer protection purposes. We first analyzed the Federal Reserve's Debit Interchange Fees and Routing Rule (Regulation II).

As part of that work, we reviewed selected statutes and regulations, analyzed available data and documents from the Federal Reserve, GAO, and market participants and experts, and interviewed agency officials and market experts. Additionally, we analyzed two SEC rules on asset-backed securities (ABS): Issuer Review of Assets in Offerings of ABS and Disclosure for ABS Required by Section 945 and 943 of the Act, respectively. To do this, we reviewed selected statutes and regulations and analyzed data on ABS issuances obtained from the Securities Industry and Financial Markets Association (SIFMA).

Lastly, we analyzed SEC's rule on Shareholder Approval of Executive Compensation and Golden Parachute Compensation. As part of that analysis, we reviewed selected regulations and analyzed available data on shareholder votes on executive compensation that we obtained from Institutional Shareholder Services, Inc., a proxy advisory firm that advises institutional investors on how to vote proxies and provides consulting services to corporations seeking to improve their corporate governance.

For all of the data described above, we assessed the reliability of the data and found it to be reliable for our purposes.

We conducted this performance audit from December 2011 to December 2012 in accordance with generally accepted government auditing standards. Those standards require that we plan and perform the audit to obtain sufficient, appropriate evidence to provide a reasonable basis for our findings and conclusions based on our audit objectives.

We believe that the evidence obtained provides a reasonable basis for our findings and conclusions based on our audit objectives.

APPENDIX II. TABLES LISTING DODD-FRANK ACT RULES EFFECTIVE AS OF JULY 23, 2012

The following table lists the Dodd-Frank Act rules that we identified as final and effective during the scope period for this review—July 21, 2011, and July 23, 2012.

Table 10. Dodd-Frank Act Rules Effective between July 21, 2011, and July 23, 2012

Rulemaking	Responsible regulator	Effective date	Did regulator identify the rule as having significant economic impact?	Did regulator quantify costs of final rule other than PRA costs?	Did regulator quantify benefits of final rule?	Did regulator qualitatively identify costs of final rule?	Did regulator qualitatively identify benefits of final rule?
Risk-Based Capital Standards: Advanced Capital Adequacy Framework—Basel II; Establishment of a Risk-Based Capital Floor	FDIC, Federal Reserve, and OCC	07/28/11	No	No[a]	No	Yes	Yes
Securities Whistleblower Incentives and Protections	SEC	08/12/11	Yes	No	No	Yes	Yes
Prohibition on the Employment, or Attempted Employment, of Manipulative and Deceptive Devices and Prohibition on Price Manipulation	CFTC	08/15/11	No	No	No	Yes	Yes
Fair Credit Reporting Risk-Based Pricing Regulations	Federal Reserve and Federal Trade Commission	08/15/11	No	No	No	Yes	Yes
Equal Credit Opportunity	Federal Reserve	08/15/11	No	No	No	Yes	Yes
Certain Orderly Liquidation Authority Provisions under Title II of the Dodd-Frank Wall Street Reform and Consumer Protection Act	FDIC	08/15/11	No	No	No	No	Yes
Public Company Accounting Oversight Board; Order Approving Proposed Board Funding Final Rules for Allocation of the Board's Accounting Support Fee Among Issuers, Brokers, and Dealers, and Other Amendments to the Board's Funding Rules	SEC	08/18/11	N/A	N/A	N/A	N/A	N/A
Authority to Designate Financial Market Utilities (FMU) as Systemically Important	FSOC	08/26/11	No	No	No	Yes	Yes
Family Offices	SEC	08/29/11	Yes	Yes	Yes	Yes	Yes
Security Ratings	SEC	09/02/11; 12/31/12	No	No	No	Yes	Yes

Rulemaking	Responsible regulator	Effective date	Did regulator identify the rule as having significant economic impact?	Did regulator quantify costs of final rule other than PRA costs?	Did regulator quantify benefits of final rule?	Did regulator qualitatively identify costs of final rule?	Did regulator qualitatively identify benefits of final rule?
Agricultural Commodity Definition	CFTC	09/12/11	No	No	No	Yes	Yes
Retail Foreign Exchange Transactions; Conforming Changes to Existing Regulations in Response to the Dodd-Frank Wall Street Reform and Consumer Protection Act	CFTC	09/12/11	No	No	No	Yes	Yes
Rules Implementing Amendments to the Investment Advisers Act of 1940	SEC	07/21/11; 09/19/11	Yes	Yes	Yes	Yes	Yes
Privacy of Consumer Financial Information; Conforming Amendments Under Dodd-Frank Act	CFTC	09/20/11	No	No	No	Yes	Yes
Large Trader Reporting for Physical Commodity Swaps	CFTC	09/20/11	No	No	No	Yes	Yes
Business Affiliate Marketing and Disposal of Consumer Information Rules	CFTC	09/20/11[b]	No	No	No	Yes	Yes
Suspension of the duty to file reports for classes of asset-backed securities	SEC	09/22/11	No	No	No	Yes	Yes
Removing Any Reference to or Reliance on Credit Ratings in Commission Regulations; Proposing Alternatives to the Use of Credit Ratings	CFTC	09/23/11	No	No	No	Yes	Yes
Process for Review of Swaps for Mandatory Clearing	CFTC	09/26/11	No	No	No	Yes	Yes
Provisions Common to Registered Entities	CFTC	09/26/11	No	No	No	Yes	Yes
Debit Card Interchange Fees and Routing	Federal Reserve	10/01/11[b]	Yes	No	No	Yes	Yes
Whistleblower Incentives and Protection	CFTC	10/24/11	Yes	No	No	Yes	Yes
Swap Data Repositories: Registration Standards, Duties and Core Principles	CFTC	10/31/11	Yes	Yes	No	Yes	Yes
Disclosure of Information; Privacy Act Regulations; Notice and Amendments	FDIC	11/14/11	N/A	N/A	N/A	N/A	N/A

Table 10. (Continued)

Rulemaking	Responsible regulator	Effective date	Did regulator identify the rule as having significant economic impact?	Did regulator quantify costs of final rule other than PRA costs?	Did regulator quantify benefits of final rule?	Did regulator qualitatively identify costs of final rule?	Did regulator qualitatively identify benefits of final rule?
Resolution Plans Required	Federal Reserve and FDIC	11/30/11	No	No	No	Yes	Yes
Remittance Transfers	NCUA	11/30/11	No	No	No	No	No
Amendment to July 14, 2011 Order for Swap Regulation	CFTC	12/23/11	No	No	No	No	Yes
Capital Plans	Federal Reserve	12/30/11	No	No	No	Yes	No
Agricultural Swaps Rule	CFTC	12/31/11	No	No	No	Yes	Yes
Derivatives Clearing Organization General Provisions and Core Principles	CFTC	01/09/12	Yes	Yes	No	Yes	Yes
Position Limits for Futures and Swaps	CFTC	01/17/12	Yes	Yes	No	Yes	Yes
Performance of Registration Functions by National Futures Association with Respect to Swap Dealers and Major Swap Participants	CFTC	01/19/12	N/A	N/A	N/A	N/A	N/A
Mine Safety Disclosure	SEC	01/27/12	No	No	No	Yes	Yes
Reporting Line for the Commission's Inspector General	SEC	02/14/12	N/A	N/A	N/A	N/A	N/A
Investment of Customer Funds and Funds Held in an Account for Foreign Futures and Foreign Options Transactions	CFTC	02/17/12	Yes	No	No	Yes	Yes
Registration of Foreign Boards of Trade	CFTC	02/21/12	No	Yes	No	Yes	Yes
Net Worth Standard for Accredited Investors	SEC	02/27/12	Yes	No	No	Yes	Yes
Real-Time Reporting of Swap Transaction Data	CFTC	03/09/12	Yes	No	No	Yes	Yes
Swap Data Recordkeeping and Reporting Requirements	CFTC	03/13/12	Yes	No	No	Yes	Yes
Registration of Swap Dealers and Major Swap Participants	CFTC	03/19/12	No	Yes	No	Yes	Yes

Rulemaking	Responsible regulator	Effective date	Did regulator identify the rule as having significant economic impact?	Did regulator quantify costs of final rule other than PRA costs?	Did regulator quantify benefits of final rule?	Did regulator qualitatively identify costs of final rule?	Did regulator qualitatively identify benefits of final rule?
Reporting by Investment Advisers to Private Funds and Certain Commodity Pool Operators and Commodity Trading Advisors on Form PF	SEC and CFTC	03/31/12	Yes	No	No	Yes	Yes
Resolution Plans Required for Insured Depository Institutions With $50 Billion or More in Total Assets	FDIC	04/01/12	No	No	No	Yes	Yes
Protection of Cleared Swaps Customer Contracts and Collateral; Conforming Amendments to the Commodity Broker Bankruptcy Provisions	CFTC	04/09/12	Yes	No	No	Yes	Yes
Exemptions for Security-Based Swaps Issued by Certain Clearing Agencies	SEC	04/16/12	No	No	No	Yes	Yes
Business Conduct Standards for Swap Dealers and Major Swap Participants	CFTC	04/17/12	Yes	No	No	Yes	Yes
Commodity Pool Operators and Commodity Trading Advisers: Compliance Obligations	CFTC	04/24/12; 07/02/12	No	Yes	No	Yes	Yes
Authority To Require Supervision and Regulation of Certain Nonbank Financial Companies	FSOC	05/11/12	No	No	No	No	Yes
Implementation of the Freedom of Information Act	FSOC	05/11/12	No	No	No	Yes	No
Investment Advisor Performance Compensation Rule	SEC	05/22/12	Yes	Yes	Yes	Yes	Yes
Mutual Insurance Holding Company Treated as Insurance Company	FDIC	05/30/12	No	No	No	No	No
Swap Dealer and Major Swap Participant Recordkeeping, Reporting, and Duties Rules; Futures Commission Merchant and Introducing Broker Conflicts of Interest Rules; and Chief Compliance Officer Rules for Swap Dealers, Major Swap Participants, and Futures Commission Merchants	CFTC	06/04/12	Yes	Yes	No	Yes	Yes
Statement of Policy Regarding the Conformance Period for Entities Engaged in Prohibited Proprietary Trading or Private Equity Fund or Hedge Fund Activities	Federal Reserve	06/08/12	N/A	N/A	N/A	N/A	N/A

Table 10. (Continued)

Rulemaking	Responsible regulator	Effective date	Did regulator identify the rule as having significant economic impact?	Did regulator quantify costs of final rule other than PRA costs?	Did regulator quantify benefits of final rule?	Did regulator qualitatively identify costs of final rule?	Did regulator qualitatively identify benefits of final rule?
Commodity Options	CFTC	06/26/12	No	No	No	Yes	Yes
State Official Notification Rule	CFPB	06/29/12	N/A	N/A	N/A	N/A	N/A
Rules Relating to Investigations	CFPB	06/29/12	N/A	N/A	N/A	N/A	N/A
Rules of Practice for Adjudication Proceedings	CFPB	06/29/12	N/A	N/A	N/A	N/A	N/A
Collection of Checks and Other Items by Federal Reserve Banks and Funds Transfers Through Fedwire: Elimination of ''As-of Adjustments'' and Other Clarifications	Federal Reserve	07/12/12	No	No	No	Yes	Yes
Assessment of Fees on Large Bank Holding Companies and Nonbank Financial Companies Supervised by the Federal Reserve Board To Cover the Expenses of the Financial Research Fund	Treasury	07/20/12	Yes	Yes	No	Yes	Yes
Supervised Securities Holding Company Registration	Federal Reserve	07/20/12	No	No	No	No	No
Alternatives to the Use of External Credit Ratings in the Regulations of the OCC	OCC	07/21/12; 01/01/13	No	No[a]	No	No	No
Permissible Investments for Federal and State Savings Associations: Corporate Debt Securities	FDIC	07/21/12	No	No	No	Yes	No
Guidance on Due Diligence Requirements for Savings Associations in Determining Whether a Corporate Debt Security Is Eligible for Investment	FDIC	07/21/12	N/A	N/A	N/A	N/A	N/A
Guidance on Due Diligence Requirements in Determining Whether Securities Are Eligible for Investment	OCC	01/01/13[c]	N/A	N/A	N/A	N/A	N/A

Rulemaking	Responsible regulator	Effective date	Did regulator identify the rule as having significant economic impact?	Did regulator quantify costs of final rule other than PRA costs?	Did regulator quantify benefits of final rule?	Did regulator qualitatively identify costs of final rule?	Did regulator qualitatively identify benefits of final rule?
Supervisory Guidance on Stress Testing for Banking Organizations With More Than $10 Billion in Total Consolidated Assets	FDIC, Federal Reserve, and OCC	07/23/12	N/A	N/A[a]	N/A	N/A	N/A
Calculation of Maximum Obligation Limitation	FDIC and Treasury	07/23/12	No	No	No	No	No
Further Definition of "Swap Dealer," "Security-Based Swap Dealer," "Major Swap Participant," "Major Security-Based Swap Participant," and "Eligible Contract Participant"	CFTC and SEC	07/23/12; 12/31/12	Yes	Yes	No	Yes	Yes

Source: GAO summary of information from the *Federal Register*, the Federal Reserve Bank of St. Louis (http://www.stlouisfed.org/regreformrules/final.aspx) and Davis Polk & Wardwell LLP.

Note: N/A refers to those rulemakings related to interpretive rules, general statements of policy, and rules that deal with agency organization, procedure, or practice, and thus not subject to Administrative Procedure Act (APA) requirements.

[a] OCC undertook an assessment of these rules, which included quantified total cost estimates, but the assessments were not published in the *Federal Register* notices.

[b] Compliance dates vary.

[c] OCC's guidance is included in this review, even though the effective date is outside our scope period, because the accompanying rule and similar FDIC guidance are included in this review.

The following table lists the Dodd-Frank Act rules that we identified as final and effective during the scope period for our first review—July 21, 2010, and July 21, 2011.

Table 11. Dodd-Frank Act Rules Effective as of July 21, 2011

Rulemaking	Responsible regulator	Effective date	Did the regulator have some level of discretion?	Did the regulator identify the rule as having significant economic impact?
Deposit Insurance Regulations; Permanent Increase in Standard Coverage Amount; Advertisement of Membership; International Banking; Foreign Banks (75 Fed. Reg. 49,363)	FDIC	8/13/2010	No	No
Display of Official Sign; Permanent Increase in Standard Maximum Share (75 Fed. Reg. 53,841)	NCUA	9/2/2010	No	No
Internal Controls over Financial Reporting in Exchange Act Periodic Reports (75 Fed. Reg. 57,385)	SEC	9/21/2010	No	No
Commission Guidance Regarding Auditing, Attestation, and Related Professional Practice Standards Related to Brokers and Dealers (75 Fed. Reg. 60,616)	SEC	10/1/2010	n/a	n/a
Removal from Regulation FD of the Exemption for Credit Rating Agencies (75 Fed. Reg. 61,050)	SEC	10/4/2010	No	No
Regulation of Off-Exchange Retail Foreign Exchange Transactions and Intermediaries (75 Fed. Reg. 55,410)	CFTC	10/18/2010	Yes	No
Deposit Insurance Regulations: Unlimited Coverage for Noninterest-Bearing Transaction Accounts (75 Fed. Reg. 69,577)	FDIC	12/31/2010	No	No
Designated Reserve Ratio (75 Fed. Reg. 79,286)	FDIC	1/1/2011	Yes	No
Rules of Practice – Handling of Proposed Rule Changes Submitted by Self-Regulatory Organizations (76 Fed. Reg. 4066)	SEC	1/24/2011	n/a	n/a
Deposit Insurance Regulations; Unlimited Coverage for Noninterest-Bearing Transaction Accounts; Inclusion of Interest on Lawyers Trust Accounts (76 Fed. Reg. 4813)	FDIC	1/27/2011	No	No
Issuer Review of Assets in Offerings of Asset-Back Securities (76 Fed. Reg. 4231)	SEC	3/28/2011	Yes	Yes

Rulemaking	Responsible regulator	Effective date	Did the regulator have some level of discretion?	Did the regulator identify the rule as having significant economic impact?
Disclosure for Asset-Backed Securities Required by Section 943 of the Dodd-Frank Wall Street Reform and Consumer Protection Act (76 Fed. Reg. 4489)	SEC	3/28/2011	Yes	Yes
Conformance Period for Entities Engaged in Prohibited Proprietary Trading or Private Equity Fund or Hedge Fund Activities (76 Fed. Reg. 8265)	Federal Reserve	4/1/2011	Yes	No
Assessments, Large Bank Pricing (76 Fed. Reg. 10,672)	FDIC	4/1/2011	Yes	No
Higher Rate Threshold for Escrow Requirements (76 Fed. Reg. 11,319)	Federal Reserve	4/1/2011	No	No
Shareholder Approval of Executive Compensation and Golden Parachute Compensation (76 Fed. Reg. 6010)	SEC	4/4/2011	Yes	Yes
Establishment of the FDIC Systemic Resolution Advisory Committee (76 Fed. Reg. 25,352)	FDIC	4/28/2011	n/a	n/a
Order Directing Funding for the Governmental Accounting Standards Board (76 Fed. Reg. 28,247)	SEC	5/16/2011	n/a	n/a
Share Insurance and Appendix (76 Fed. Reg. 30,250)	NCUA	6/24/2011	No	No
Modification of Treasury Regulations Pursuant to Section 939A of the Dodd- Frank Wall Street Reform and Consumer Protection Act (76 Fed. Reg. 39,278)	Treasury	7/6/2011	No	No
Retail Foreign Exchange Transactions (76 Fed. Reg. 40,779)	FDIC	7/15/2011	Yes	No
Retail Foreign Exchange Transactions (76 Fed. Reg. 41,375)	OCC	7/15/2011	Yes	No
Beneficial Ownership Reporting Requirements and Security-Based Swaps (76 Fed. Reg. 34,579)	SEC	7/16/2011	Yes	No
Prohibition Against Payment of Interest on Demand Deposits (76 Fed. Reg. 42,015)	Federal Reserve	7/21/2011	No	No

Table 11. (Continued)

Rulemaking	Responsible regulator	Effective date	Did the regulator have some level of discretion?	Did the regulator identify the rule as having significant economic impact?
List of OTS Regulations to be Enforced by the OCC and FDIC Pursuant to the Dodd-Frank Act (76 Fed. Reg. 39,246)	OCC/FDIC	7/21/2011	n/a	n/a
Office of Thrift Supervision Integration; Dodd-Frank Act Implementation (76 Fed. Reg. 43,549)	OCC	7/21/2011	n/a	n/a
Exemptions for Advisers to Venture Capital Funds, Private Fund Advisers With Less Than $150 Million in Assets Under Management, and Foreign Private Advisers (76 Fed. Reg. 39,646)	SEC	7/21/2011	Yes	No
Consumer Transfer Protection Date (75 Fed. Reg. 57,252)	CFPB	7/21/2011	n/a	n/a
Identification of Enforceable Rules and Orders (76 Fed. Reg. 43,569)	CFPB	7/21/2011	n/a	n/a
Consumer Leasing – Exempt Consumer Credit under Regulation M (75 Fed. Reg. 18,349)	Federal Reserve	7/21/2011	No	No
Truth in Lending – Exempt Consumer Credit under Regulation Z (76 Fed. Reg. 18,354)	Federal Reserve	7/21/2011	No	No
Interest on Deposits; Deposit Insurance Coverage (76 Fed. Reg. 41,392)	FDIC	7/21/2011	No	No

Source: GAO summary of information from the *Federal Register* and Federal Reserve Bank of St. Louis (http://www.stlouisfed.org/regreformrules/final.aspx).

Note: N/A refers to those rulemakings related to interpretive rules, general statements of policy, and rules that deal with agency organization, procedure, or practice, and thus not subject to APA requirements. In some instances, we found that an agency had discretion to implement the statute, even though the discretion was limited, because the exercise of discretion was important to implementation.

Appendix III. Summary of Rulemakings Related to the Dodd-Frank Act Provisions Applicable to Systemically Important Financial Institutions

The Dodd-Frank Act contains several provisions that apply to nonbank financial companies designated by the Financial Stability Oversight Council for Federal Reserve supervision and enhanced prudential standards (nonbank SIFI) and bank holding companies with $50 billion or more in total consolidated assets (bank SIFI). Table 12 summarizes those provisions and the rulemakings, including their status, to implement those provisions.

Table 12. Rulemakings Implementing the Dodd-Frank Act Provisions Applicable to Systemically Important Financial Institutions and Their Status as of October 12, 2012

Dodd-Frank Act provision	Rulemaking status
FSOC designation of Nonbanks for Federal Reserve supervision—Section 113 authorizes FSOC to determine that a nonbank financial company shall be subject to enhanced prudential standards and supervision by the Federal Reserve if FSOC determines that the company could pose a threat to the financial stability of the U.S.	FSOC final rule 77 Fed. Reg. 21,637 (Apr. 11, 2012)
FSOC's final rule describes the manner in which FSOC intends to apply the statutory standards (for size, interconnectedness, complexity, leverage, and liquidity), and the procedures FSOC intends to follow when making a determination to designate a nonbank financial institution for Federal Reserve supervision under section 113 of the act.	FSOC has not yet designated any nonbank finan-cial companies for Federal Reserve supervision
Enhanced supervision and prudential standards—Sections 165 and 166 require the Federal Reserve to impose enhanced prudential standards and early remediation requirements on bank holding companies with $50 billion or more in total consolidated assets and nonbank financial companies designated by FSOC to prevent or mitigate risks to U.S. financial stability.[a]	Federal Reserve proposed rule 77 Fed. Reg. 594 (Jan. 5, 2012)[b]
Enhanced risk-based capital and leverage requirements required under section 165(b)(1)(A)(i)—capital plans: Bank holding companies with $50 billion or more in total consolidated assets and nonbank financial companies designated by FSOC would be subject to the Federal Reserve's capital plan rule, which requires companies to submit an annual capital plan to the Board for review that, together with the proposed stress tests (below), would demonstrate to the Board that the company has robust, forward-looking capital	proposal included in Jan. 5, 2012 proposed rule

Table 12. (Continued)

Dodd-Frank Act provision	Rulemaking status
planning processes that account for their unique risks and permit continued operations during times of stress.[c]	
Enhanced risk-based capital and leverage requirements required under section 165(b)(1)(A)(i)—capital surcharges: The Federal Reserve intends to issue a proposal imposing a quantitative risk-based capital surcharge for all or a subgroup of bank holding companies with $50 billion or more in total consolidated assets and nonbank financial companies designated by FSOC based on the Basel capital surcharge for Globally Systemically Important Banks (G-SIBs).[d]	intention included in Jan. 5, 2012 proposed rule
Enhanced liquidity requirements required under section 165(b)(1)(A)(ii)—liquidity risk management standards: Bank holding companies with $50 billion or more in total consolidated assets and nonbank financial companies designated by FSOC would be subject to liquidity risk management standards that require the companies, among other things, to project cash flow needs over various time horizons, stress test the projections at least monthly, determine a liquidity buffer, and maintain a contingency funding plan that identifies potential sources of liquidity strain and alternative sources of funding.	proposal included in Jan. 5, 2012 proposed rule
Enhanced liquidity requirements required under Section 165(b)(1)(A)(ii)—Basel liquidity ratios: The Federal Reserve intends to issue a proposal imposing quantitative liquidity requirements on all or a subgroup of bank holding companies with $50 billion or more in total consolidated assets and nonbank financial companies designated by FSOC based on Basel III liquidity ratios.	intention included in Jan. 5, 2012 proposed rule
Credit exposure reports required under section 165(d)(2): Section 165 also requires the Federal Reserve and the Federal Deposit Insurance Corporation (FDIC) to impose credit exposure reporting requirements on bank holding companies with $50 billion or more in total consolidated assets and nonbank financial companies designated by FSOC. The joint proposed rule would require the companies to report significant exposures to other covered companies and significant exposures that other covered companies have to that company	Federal Reserve and FDIC proposed rule 76 Fed. Reg. 22,648 (Apr. 22, 2011)
Concentration limits required under section 165(e): As required by the act, the Federal Reserve would prohibit a bank holding company with $50 billion or more in total consolidated assets or a nonbank financial company designated by FSOC from having credit exposure to any unaffiliated company that exceeds 25 percent of the company's capital stock and surplus. The Federal Reserve proposed a more stringent credit exposure limit of 10 percent between the largest, more complex financial institutions.	proposal included in January 5, 2012 proposed rule

Dodd-Frank Act provision	Rulemaking status
Stress Tests required under section 165(i): Bank holding companies with $50 billion or more in total consolidated assets and nonbank financial companies designated by FSOC are required by the act to conduct semi-annual company-run stress tests, and the Federal Reserve is required to conduct an annual stress test on each of the companies[e] The final rule builds on the stress tests required under the capital plans that large, complex bank holding companies submitted to the Federal Reserve for supervision under the Supervisory Capital Assessment Program (SCAP) in 2009, the subsequent Comprehensive Capital and Analysis Review (CCAR) in 2011, and the capital plan rule effective Dec. 30, 2011.	Federal Reserve final rule 77 Fed. Reg. 62,378 (Oct. 12, 2012)
Resolution plans required under section 165(d)(1): Section 165 also requires the Federal Reserve and the Federal Deposit Insurance Corporation (FDIC) to require resolution plans from bank holding companies with $50 billion or more in total consolidated assets and nonbank financial companies designated by FSOC. The joint final rule requires each plan to include, among other things, information about the company's ownership structure, core business lines, and critical operations, and a strategic analysis of how the SIFI can be resolved under the U.S. Bankruptcy Code in a way that would not pose systemic risk to the financial system[f]	Federal Reserve and FDIC final rule 76 Fed. Reg. 67,323 (Nov. 1, 2011)
Debt-to-Equity Limits under section 165(j): Section 165(j) provides that the Federal Reserve must require a bank holding company with $50 billion or more in total consolidated assets or a nonbank financial company designated by FSOC to maintain a debt-to-equity ratio of no more than 15-to-1, upon a determination by the Council that (i) such company poses a grave threat to the financial stability of the United States and (ii) the imposition of such a requirement is necessary to mitigate the risk that the company poses to U.S. financial stability	proposal included in Jan. 5, 2012 proposed rule
Early remediation requirements under section 166: Section 166 requires the Federal Reserve, in consultation with FSOC and FDIC, to prescribe regulations to provide for the early remediation of financial distress of bank holding companies with $50 billion or more in total consolidated assets and nonbank financial companies designated by FSOC. The proposed requirements would include a number of triggers for remediation, including capital levels, stress test results, and risk management weaknesses. In certain situations, the Federal Reserve would impose restrictions on growth, assets, acquisitions, capital distributions and executive compensation, and other activities that the Federal Reserve deems appropriate.	proposal included in Jan. 5, 2012 proposed rule
FDIC Orderly Liquidation Authority—Title II gives the FDIC new orderly liquidation authority to act as a receiver of troubled nonbank financial companies designated by FSOC.	FDIC final rule 76 Fed. Reg. 41,626 (July 15, 2011)

Table 12. (Continued)

Dodd-Frank Act provision	Rulemaking status
The FDIC has issued and expects to issue a number of rules to exercise this new authority. The FDIC indicated that the July 15, 2011 rule represents the culmination of the initial phase of such rulemaking.	
Federal Reserve authority to impose mitigatory actions on certain companies determined to pose a grave threat to financial stability—Section 121(a) allows the Federal Reserve, with a two-thirds vote by FSOC, to impose certain additional restrictions on bank holding companies with $50 billion or more in total consolidated assets and nonbank financial companies designated by FSOC determined to pose a grave threat to the financial stability of the United States, including limiting mergers and acquisitions, requiring the company to terminate activities, or requiring the company to sell or transfer assets or off-balance-sheet items to unaffiliated entities.	No rules issued
Collins Amendment—Section 171(b) requires the appropriate federal banking agencies to establish permanent minimum risk-based capital and leverage floors on insured depository institutions, depository institution holding companies, and nonbank financial companies designated by FSOC.	Federal Reserve, FDIC, and OCC final rule
Under the final rule, these institutions must calculate their floors using the minimum risk-based capital and leverage requirements under the prompt corrective action framework implementing section 38 of the Federal Deposit Insurance Act, which currently are Basel I's general risk-based capital rules.	76 Fed. Reg. 37,620 (June 28,2011)
Concentration Limit/ liability cap on large financial institutions—Section 622 establishes, subject to recommendations by FSOC, a financial sector concentration limit that generally prohibits a financial company from merging or consolidating with, acquiring all or substantially all of the assets of, or otherwise acquiring control of, another company if the resulting company's consolidated liabilities would exceed 10 percent of the aggregate consolidated liabilities of all financial companies.[g]	No rules issued

Source: Dodd-Frank Act, *Federal Register*, and other documents from regulators and FSOC.

[a] Section 165 also directs the Federal Reserve to impose enhanced prudential standards for bank holding companies with $50 billion or more in total consolidated assets and nonbank financial companies designated by FSOC regarding overall risk management, which also were proposed in the January 5, 2012, rule. Additionally, section 115 also authorizes FSOC to recommend additional enhanced prudential standards for bank holding companies with $50 billion or more in total consolidated assets and nonbank financial companies designated by FSOC to the Federal Reserve.

[b] In this January 5, 2012, proposed rule, the Federal Reserve proposed rules to implement certain but not all of the requirements of sections 165 and 166 of the Dodd-Frank Act.

[c] Bank SIFIs are already required to comply with the capital plan rule. The Federal Reserve issued its final capital plans rule on December 1, 2011 (76 Fed. Reg. 74,631).

[d] In November 2011, the Financial Stability Board (FSB) identified 29 G-SIBs and indicated it would update this list annually each November. FSB updated this list on November 1, 2012. The updated list contains 28 G-SIBs; the same eight U.S. bank SIFIs were designated as G-SIBs in 2011 and 2012. Additionally, on November 1, 2012, FSB allocated each G-SIB into a bucket corresponding to its different levels of capital surcharge.

[e] Section 165(i)(2) of the Act requires that any financial company with more than $10 billion in total consolidated assets and that is regulated by a federal financial regulatory agency also be subject to company-run stress tests. The Federal Reserve issued a separate rule to implement this requirement. 77 Fed. Reg. 62,396 (Oct. 12, 2012).

[f] Bank SIFIs with at least $250 billion in total nonbank assets were required to submit their first resolution plans by July 1, 2012.

[g] FSOC finalized a report and issued recommendations on implementing this provision. FSOC asked for comments on its recommendations. Financial Stability Oversight Council, *Study & Recommendations Regarding Concentration Limits on Large Financial Companies* (Washington, D.C.: January 2011).

APPENDIX IV. ECONOMETRIC ANALYSES OF THE IMPACT OF ENHANCED REGULATION AND OVERSIGHT ON SIFIS

Methodology

We conducted an econometric analysis to assess the impact of the Dodd-Frank Act's new requirements for bank SIFIs on (1) the cost of credit they provide and (2) their safety and soundness. Our multivariate econometric model used a difference-in-difference design that exploits the fact that the Dodd-Frank Act subjects bank holding companies with total consolidated assets of $50 billion or more to enhanced regulation by the Federal Reserve but not others, so we can view bank holding companies with total consolidated assets of $50 billion or more (bank SIFIs) as the treatment group and other bank holding companies as the control group. We compared the changes in the characteristics of U.S. bank SIFIs over time to changes in the characteristics of other U.S. bank holding companies over time. All else being equal, the difference in the differences is the impact of new requirements for bank SIFIs primarily tied to enhanced regulation and oversight under the Federal Reserve. Our general regression specification is the following:

$$y_{bq} = \alpha_b + \beta_q + \gamma_q SIFI_{bq} + X'_{bq}\Theta + \varepsilon_{bq}$$

where *b* denotes the bank holding company, q denotes the quarter, y_{bq} is the dependent variable, α_b is a bank holding company-specific intercept, β_q is a quarter-specific intercept, $SIFI_{bq}$ is an indicator variable that equals 1 if bank holding company b is a SIFI in quarter q and 0 otherwise, X_{bq} is a list of other independent variables, and ε_{bq} is an error term. We estimated the parameters of the model using quarterly data on top-tier bank holding companies for the period from the first quarter of 2006 to the second quarter of 2012.

The parameters of interest are the γ_q, the coefficients on the SIFI indicators in the quarters starting with the treatment start date of the third quarter of 2010 through the second quarter of 2012. The Dodd-Frank Act was enacted in July 2010 (the third quarter of 2010), so the SIFI indicator is equal to zero for all bank holding companies for all quarters from the first quarter of 2006 to the second quarter of 2010. The SIFI indicator is equal to 1 for all bank holding companies with assets of $50 billion or more for the third quarter of 2010 through the second quarter of 2012 and the SIFI indicator is equal to zero for all other bank holding companies for those quarters. Thus, for quarters from the third of 2010 to the second of 2012, the parameter γ_q measures the average difference in the dependent variable between bank SIFIs and other bank holding companies in those quarters relative to the base quarter.

We use different dependent variables (y_{bq}) to estimate the impacts of the new requirements for SIFIs on the cost of credit provided by bank SIFIs and on various aspects of bank SIFIs' safety and soundness, including capital adequacy, asset quality, earnings, and liquidity.

- **Funding cost.** A bank holding company's funding cost is the cost of deposits or liabilities that it then uses to make loans or otherwise acquire assets. More specifically, a bank holding company's funding cost is the interest rate it pays when it borrows funds. All else being equal, the greater a bank holding company's funding cost, the greater the interest rate it charges when it makes loans. We measure funding cost as an institution's interest expense as a percent of interest-bearing liabilities.

- **Capital adequacy.** Capital absorbs losses, promotes public confidence, helps restrict excessive asset growth, and provides protection to creditors. We use two alternative measures of capital adequacy: tangible common equity as a percent of total assets and tangible common equity as a percent of risk-weighted assets.
- **Asset quality.** Asset quality reflects the quantity of existing and potential credit risk associated with the institution's loan and investment portfolios and other assets, as well as off-balance sheet transactions. Asset quality also reflects the ability of management to identify and manage credit risk. We measure asset quality as performing assets as a percent of total assets, where performing assets are equal to total assets less assets 90 days or more past due and still accruing interest, assets in non-accrual status, and other real estate owned.
- **Earnings.** Earnings are the initial safeguard against the risks of engaging in the banking business and represent the first line of defense against capital depletion that can result from declining asset values. We measure earnings as net income as a percent of total assets.
- **Liquidity.** Liquidity represents the ability to fund assets and meet obligations as they become due, and liquidity risk is the risk of not being able to obtain funds at a reasonable price within a reasonable time period to meet obligations as they become due. We use two different variables to measure liquidity. The first variable is liquid assets as a percent of volatile liabilities. This variable is similar in spirit to the liquidity coverage ratio introduced by the Basel Committee on Banking Supervision and measures a bank holding company's capacity to meet its liquidity needs under a significantly severe liquidity stress scenario. We measure liquid assets as the sum of cash and balances due from depository institutions, securities (less pledged securities), federal funds sold and reverse repurchases, and trading assets. We measure volatile liabilities as the sum of federal funds purchased and repurchase agreements, trading liabilities (less derivatives with negative fair value), other borrowed funds, deposits held in foreign offices, and large time deposits held in domestic offices. Large time deposits are defined as time deposits greater than $100,000 prior to March 2010 and as time deposits greater than $250,000 in and after March 2010.

- The second liquidity variable is stable liabilities as a percent of total liabilities. This variable measures the extent to which a bank holding company relies on stable funding sources to finance its assets and activities. This variable is related in spirit to the net stable funding ratio introduced by the Basel Committee on Banking Supervision, which measures the amount of stable funding based on the liquidity characteristics of an institution's assets and activities over a 1 year horizon. We measure stable funding as total liabilities minus volatile liabilities as described earlier.

Finally, we include a limited number of independent variables (X^{bq}) to control for things that may differentially affect SIFIs and non-SIFIs in the quarters since the Dodd-Frank Act was enacted. We include these variables to reduce the likelihood that our estimates of the impact of new requirements for SIFIs are reflecting something other than the impact of the Dodd-Frank Act's new requirements for SIFIs.

- **Nontraditional income.** Nontraditional income generally captures income from capital market activities. Bank holding companies with more nontraditional income are likely to have different business models than those with more income from traditional banking activities. Changes in capital markets in the period since the Dodd-Frank Act was enacted may have had a greater effect on bank holding companies with more nontraditional income. If bank SIFIs typically have more nontraditional income than other bank holding companies, then changes in capital markets in the time since the Dodd-Frank Act was enacted may have differentially affected the two groups. We measure nontraditional income as the sum of trading revenue; investment banking, advisory, brokerage, and underwriting fees and commissions; venture capital revenue; insurance commissions and fees; and interest income from trading assets less associated interest expense, and we express nontraditional income as a percent of operating revenue.
- **Securitization income.** Bank holding companies with more income from securitization are likely to have different business models than those with more income from traditional banking associated with an originate-to-hold strategy for loans. Changes in the market for securitized products in the period since the Dodd-Frank Act was enacted may thus have had a greater effect on bank holding

companies with more securitization income. If bank SIFIs typically have more securitization income than other bank holding companies, then changes in the market for securitized products in the time since the Dodd-Frank Act was enacted may have differentially affected the two groups. We measure securitization income as the sum of net servicing fees, net securitization income, and interest and dividend income on mortgage-backed securities minus associated interest expense, and we express securitization as a percent of operating revenue. Operating revenue is the sum of interest income and noninterest income less interest expense and loan loss provisions.

- **Foreign exposure.** Changes in other countries, such as the sovereign debt crisis in Europe, may have a larger effect on bank holding companies with more foreign exposure. If bank SIFIs typically have more foreign exposure than other bank holding companies, then changes in foreign markets may have differentially affected the two groups. We measure foreign exposure as the sum of foreign debt securities (held-to-maturity and available-for-sale), foreign bank loans, commercial and industrial loans to non-U.S. addresses, and foreign government loans. We express foreign exposure as a percent of total assets.
- **Size.** We include size because bank SIFIs tend to be larger than other bank holding companies, and market pressures or other forces not otherwise accounted for may have differentially affected large and small bank holding companies in the time since the Dodd-Frank Act was enacted. We measure the size of a bank holding company as the natural logarithm of its total assets.
- **TARP participation.** We control for whether or not a bank holding company participated in the Troubled Asset Relief Program (TARP) to differentiate any impact that this program may have had from the impact of the Dodd-Frank Act.

We also conducted several sets of robustness checks:

- We restricted our sample to the set of institutions with assets that are "close" to the $50 billion cutoff for enhanced prudential regulation for bank SIFIs. Specifically, we analyzed two restricted samples of bank holding companies: (1) bank holding companies with assets between $1 billion and $100 billion and (2) bank holding companies with assets between $25 billion and $75 billion.

- We examined different treatment start dates. Specifically, we allowed the Dodd-Frank Act's new requirements for SIFIs to have an impact in 2009q3, 1 year prior to the passage of the act. We did so to allow for the possibility that institutions began to react to the act's requirements in anticipation of the act being passed.
- We analyzed alternative measures of capital adequacy, including equity capital as a percent of total assets and Tier 1 capital as a percent of risk-weighted assets.
- We analyzed commercial banks and savings banks (banks). In this case, we identified a bank as a SIFI if it is a subsidiary of a SIFI bank holding company.

Data

We conducted our analysis using quarterly data on bank holding companies from the Federal Reserve Board and SNL Financial for the period from the first quarter of 2006 to the second quarter of 2012. We also used quarterly data on commercial banks and savings banks from the Federal Deposit Insurance Corporation (FDIC), Federal Financial Institutions Exanimation Council (FFIEC), and SNL Financial for the same time period for one of our robustness checks.

Results

The Dodd-Frank Act appears to be associated with an increase in bank SIFIs' funding costs in the second quarter of 2012, but not in other quarters (see table 13). Over the period from the third quarter of 2010 to the second quarter of 2012, bank SIFIs' funding costs ranged from about 0.02 percentage points lower to about 0.05 percentage points higher than they otherwise would have been since the Dodd-Frank Act. As a group, the estimates are jointly significant. However, the individual estimates are not significantly different from zero for quarters other than the second quarter of 2012. These estimates suggest that the Dodd-Frank Act's new requirements for SIFIs have had little effect on bank SIFIs' funding costs. To the extent that borrowing costs are a function of funding costs, the new requirements for SIFIs likely have had little effect on the cost of credit thus far.[125]

Table 13. Estimated Impacts of the Dodd-Frank Act on Bank SIFIs, from Third Quarter of 2010 through Second Quarter of 2012 (percentage points)

	Cost of credit indicator	Safety and soundness indicators					
	Funding cost	Capital adequacy		Asset quality	Earnings	Liquidity	
	Interest expense (% interest-bearing liabilities)	Tangible common equity (% assets)	Tangible common equity (% risk-weighted assets)	Performing assets (% assets)	Net income (% assets)	Liquid assets (% volatile liabilities)	Stable liabilities (% liabilities)
2010 Q3	-0.02	1.16**	1.70**	1.04**	0.14**	3.58	3.64**
	(0.02)	(0.20)	(0.30)	(0.19)	(0.04)	(6.41)	(0.92)
2010 Q4	0.00	1.54**	2.21**	1.20**	0.24**	4.19	3.79**
	(0.02)	(0.23)	(0.36)	(0.19)	(0.05)	(6.55)	(0.97)
2011 Q1	0.02	1.58**	2.19**	1.26**	0.13**	-4.89	2.82**
	(0.02)	(0.24)	(0.39)	(0.20)	(0.04)	(6.70)	(1.02)
2011 Q2	0.03	1.46**	2.02**	1.32**	0.11**	-2.68	3.54**
	(0.02)	(0.24)	(0.39)	(0.21)	(0.04)	(7.17)	(1.02)
2011 Q3	0.01	1.42**	1.96**	1.30**	0.10**	2.25	5.22**
	(0.02)	(0.25)	(0.38)	(0.21)	(0.04)	(8.19)	(1.10)
2011 Q4	0.02	1.47**	1.98**	1.16**	-0.00	-4.26	5.67**
	(0.02)	(0.26)	(0.43)	(0.22)	(0.10)	(9.20)	(1.22)
2012 Q1	0.03	1.66**	2.17**	1.19**	0.03	-2.15	5.14**
	(0.02)	(0.25)	(0.41)	(0.21)	(0.04)	(10.89)	(1.27)
2012 Q2	0.05**	1.63**	2.24**	1.17**	-0.01	-2.63	5.29**
	(0.02)	(0.28)	(0.50)	(0.23)	(0.04)	(10.60)	(1.22)

Table 13. (Continued)

	Cost of credit indicator	Safety and soundness indicators					
	Funding cost	Capital adequacy		Asset quality	Earnings	Liquidity	
	Interest expense (% interest-bearing liabilities)	Tangible common equity (% assets)	Tangible common equity (% risk-weighted assets)	Performing assets (% assets)	Net income (% assets)	Liquid assets (% volatile liabilities)	Stable liabilities (% liabilities)
Number of observations	25,953	25,953	25,953	25,953	25,953	25,953	25,953
Within R-squared	0.92	0.06	0.10	0.38	0.16	0.22	0.20
Number of bank holding companies	1,374	1,374	1,374	1,374	1,374	1,374	1,374
All impacts jointly significant?	Yes	Yes	Yes	Yes	Yes	Yes	Yes

Source: GAO analysis of data from the Federal Reserve and SNL Financial.

Notes: Estimated impacts are on the variable in the column header for the quarter in the row header. Robust standard errors are in parentheses. We analyzed data for bank holding companies for the period from the first quarter of 2006 to the second quarter of 2012. We estimated the impact of the new requirements for bank SIFIs by regressing the variables listed in the table on indicators for each bank holding company in the sample, indicators for each quarter, indicators for whether or not a bank holding company is a SIFI for the period from the third quarter of 2010 to the second quarter of 2012, and other variables controlling for size, foreign exposure, securitization income, other nontraditional income, and participation in the Troubled Asset Relief Program. Estimated impacts are the coefficients on the indicators for whether or not a bank holding company is a SIFI for quarters from the third of 2010 to the second of 2012. We used an F-test to assess whether the coefficients on the SIFI indicators for all quarters are jointly significant. We used t-tests to assess whether the coefficient on the SIFI indicator for a specific quarter is significant. We used the 5 percent level as our criteria for both joint and individual significance. **=statistically significant at the 5 percent level.

Our results suggest that the Dodd-Frank Act is associated with improvements in most aspects of bank SIFIs' safety and soundness. Bank SIFIs appear to be holding more capital than they otherwise would have held since the Dodd-Frank Act was enacted. The quality of assets on the balance sheets of bank SIFIs also seems to have improved since enactment. The act is associated with higher earnings for bank SIFIs in the first four quarters after enactment. It is also associated with improved liquidity as measured by the extent to which a bank holding company is using stable sources of funding. Only liquidity measured by the capacity of a bank holding company's liquid assets to cover its volatile liabilities has not clearly improved since the enactment of the act. Thus, the Dodd- Frank Act appears to be broadly associated with improvements in most indicators of safety and soundness for bank SIFIs.

Our approach allows us to partially differentiate changes in funding costs, capital adequacy, asset quality, earnings, and liquidity associated with the Dodd-Frank Act from changes due to other factors. However, several factors make isolating and measuring the impact of the Dodd-Frank Act's new requirements for SIFIs challenging. The effects of the Dodd-Frank Act cannot be differentiated from simultaneous changes in economic conditions, such as the pace of the recovery from the recent recession, or regulations, such as those stemming from Basel III, that may differentially affect bank SIFIs and other bank holding companies. In addition, many of the new requirements for SIFIs have yet to be implemented. For example, the Federal Reserve has indicated that it will impose a capital surcharge and liquidity ratios on at least some SIFIs, but the exact form and scope of these requirements is not yet known. Nevertheless, our estimates are suggestive of the initial effects of the Dodd-Frank Act on bank SIFIs and provide a baseline against which to compare future trends.

The results of our robustness checks are as follows:

- Our results are generally robust to restricting the set of bank holding companies we analyze to those with assets of \$1 billion-\$100 billion.
- Our results are not generally robust to restricting the set of bank holding companies we analyze to those with assets of \$25 billion-\$75 billion, but this is likely to be a result of the small number of bank holding companies (29) that fit this criteria.
- Our results are generally robust to starting the "treatment" in 2009 Q3, 1 year prior to the passage of the Dodd-Frank Act. In addition, our estimates suggest that the impact of new requirements for SIFIs of

the Dodd-Frank Act may have preceded the enactment of the act itself. This finding is consistent with the theory that bank holding companies began to change their behavior in anticipation of the act's requirements, perhaps as information about the content of the act became available and the likelihood of its passage increased. However, there may be other explanations, including anticipation of Basel III requirements, reactions to stress tests, and market pressures to improve capital adequacy and liquidity.

- Our results for the impact on capital adequacy are generally similar for alternative measures of capital adequacy.
- Our results for banks' funding costs, asset quality, earnings, and liquidity as measured by liquid assets as a percent of volatile liabilities were generally similar to our baseline results for bank holding companies, but our results for capital adequacy and liquidity as measured by stable liabilities as a percent of total liabilities were not. The differences may reflect the impact of nonbank subsidiaries on bank holding companies or a number of other factors.

APPENDIX V. IMPACT ANALYSIS OF THE DEBIT CARD INTERCHANGE FEES AND ROUTING RULE

The Federal Reserve's adoption of Regulation II (Debit Card Interchange Fees and Routing), which implements section 1075 of the Dodd-Frank Act, generally has reduced debit card interchange fees.[126] However, debit card issuers, payment card networks, and merchants are continuing to adjust strategically to the rule; thus, the rule's impact has not yet been fully realized. Typically, consumers use debit cards as a cashless form of payment that electronically accesses funds from a cardholder's bank account. A consumer using a debit card authenticates and completes a transaction by entering a personal identification number (PIN) or a signature. The parties involved in a debit card transaction are (1) the customer or debit cardholder; (2) the bank that issued the debit card to the customer (issuer bank); (3) the merchant; (4) the merchant's bank (called the acquirer bank); and (4) the payment card network that processes the transaction between the merchant acquirer bank and the issuer bank. In a debit transaction, the merchant receives the amount of the purchase minus a fee that it must pay to its acquirer bank. This fee includes the debit interchange fee that the acquirer bank pays to the issuer bank.[127]

Interchange fees generally combine an ad-valorem component, which depends on the amount of the transaction, and a fixed- fee component.[128] Additionally, before Regulation II was implemented, fees varied more widely based on, among other things, the type of merchant.[129]

Although payment card networks do not receive the debit interchange fees, they set the fees. Debit cards represent a two-sided market that involves cardholders and merchants.[130] Cardholders benefit if their cards are accepted by a wide range of merchants, and merchants benefit if their ability to accept cards results in higher sales. In theory, a card network sets its interchange fees to balance the demand on the two sides of the market. It sets interchange fees high enough to attract issuers to issue debit cards processed by the network but low enough for merchants to be willing to accept the debit cards.[131] Before the enactment of section 1075 of the Dodd-Frank Act, debit interchange fees had been increasing, creating controversy in the industry about the appropriate level of debit interchange fees in the United States, which some have stated were among the highest in the world.[132] For example, some merchants stated that network competition led to higher, not lower, interchange fees as networks strived to attract issuer banks (who ultimately receive interchange fee revenue).

Section 1075 amends the Electronic Fund Transfer Act (EFTA) by adding a new section 920 regarding interchange transaction fees and rules for payment card transactions. As required by EFTA section 920, Regulation II establishes standards for assessing whether debit card interchange fees received by issuers are reasonable and proportional to the costs incurred by issuers for electronic debit transactions. The rule sets a cap on the maximum permissible interchange fee that an issuer may receive for an electronic debit transaction at $0.21 per transaction, plus 5 basis points multiplied by the transaction's value.[133] An issuer bank that complies with Regulation II's fraud-prevention standards may receive no more than an additional 1 cent per transaction.[134] The fee cap became effective on October 1, 2011. However, as required by EFTA section 920, the rule exempts from the fee cap issuers that have, together with their affiliates, less than $10 billion in assets, and transactions made using debit cards issued pursuant to government-administered payment programs or certain reloadable prepaid cards. In addition, Regulation II prohibits issuers and card networks from restricting the number of networks over which electronic debit transactions may be processed to less than two unaffiliated networks.[135] This prohibition became effective on April 1, 2012. The rule further prohibits issuers and networks from inhibiting a merchant from directing the routing of an electronic debit transaction over any network allowed by the issuer.[136] This prohibition became effective October 1, 2011.

Initial Impact on Large and Small Banks

Thus far, large banks that issue debit cards have experienced a decline in their debit interchange fees as a result of Regulation II, but small banks generally have not. As noted above, issuers that, together with their affiliates, have $10 billion or more in assets are subject to the debit card interchange fee cap. According to the Federal Reserve, 568 banks were subject to the fee cap in 2012 (covered issuers).[137] Issuers below the $10 billion asset threshold are exempt from the fee cap (exempt issuers). According to the Federal Reserve, over 14,300 banks, credit unions, savings and loans, and savings banks were exempt from the fee cap in 2012.[138]

Initial data collected by the Federal Reserve indicate that covered issuers have experienced a significant decline in their debit interchange fees and fee income as a result of Regulation II. Data published by the Federal Reserve show that 15 of 16 card networks provided a lower interchange fee, on average, to covered issuers after the rule took effect.[139] Specifically, the data show that the average interchange fee received by covered issuers declined 52 percent, from $0.50 in the first three quarters of 2011 to $0.24 in the fourth quarter. During the same period, the interchange fee as a percentage of the average transaction value for covered issuers declined from 1.29 percent to 0.60 percent.

Our own analysis also suggests that the fee cap is associated with reduced interchange fee income for covered banks.[140] To further assess the impact of the fee cap on covered banks, we conducted an econometric analysis of debit and credit card interchange fee income earned by banks from the first quarter of 2008 through the second quarter of 2012. As discussed, Regulation II subjects covered issuers but not exempt issuers to the fee cap. This allows us to compare the incomes earned by covered and exempt banks before and after the fee cap's effective date in the fourth quarter of 2011. All else being equal, the post- cap changes in income among the two groups can be inferred as the effect of the fee cap on interchange fee income earned by covered banks. Our estimates suggest that interchange fees collected by covered banks, as a percent of their assets, were about 0.007 to 0.008 percentage points lower than they otherwise would have been in the absence of the fee cap. For a bank with assets of $50 billion, this amounts to $3.5 million to $4 million in reduced interchange fee income.

In comparison, Regulation II's fee cap appears initially to have had a limited impact on exempt issuers. As we recently reported, initial data collected by the Federal Reserve indicate that card networks largely have adopted a two-tiered interchange fee structure after the implementation of Regulation II, to the benefit of exempt issuers.[141] Data published by the Federal Reserve from 16 card networks show 15 of 16 card networks provided a higher interchange fee, on average, to exempt issuers than covered issuers after the rule took effect.[142] The data further showed that the average interchange fee received by exempt issuers declined by $0.02, or around 5 percent, after the rule took effect—declining from $0.45 over the first three quarters of 2011 to $0.43 in the fourth quarter of 2011.[143] Over the same period, the interchange fee as a percentage of the average transaction value for exempt issuers declined from 1.16 to 1.10 percent.[144]

Although the fee cap appeared to have a limited impact on exempt issuers, such issuers remain concerned about the potential for their interchange fee income to decline over the long term. For example, some have noted that (1) the prohibition on network exclusivity and routing restrictions may lead networks to lower their interchange fees, in part to encourage merchants to route debit card transactions through their networks; or (2) economic forces may cause networks not to maintain a two-tiered fee structure that provides a meaningful differential between fees for exempt and covered issuers. However, some merchants and others have noted that major card networks have adopted a two-tiered fee structure and have an incentive to maintain that structure to attract exempt issuers.[145]

Impact on Merchants and Consumers

Regulation II's fee cap generally has reduced debit card interchange fees, which likely has resulted or will result in savings for merchants. According to the Federal Reserve and industry experts, the merchant acquirer market is competitive. Thus, the decrease in interchange fees likely has translated or will translate into lower merchant acquirer fees. Some noted that large merchants likely reaped immediate benefits from the fee cap, because their acquirer fees probably were reduced when interchange fees declined. In contrast, they noted that smaller merchants often opt for blended fee structures under which, for example, the merchants may be charged a flat fee per electronic payment transaction and, thus, not immediately receive the benefit of decreases in interchange fees because merchants may still be locked into contracts that have these fee structures.[146] In either case, competition in the supply of acquirer services is expected to cause acquirer banks to adjust the fees they charge to merchants and pass on any savings to avoid losing merchant business.

In its final rule, the Federal Reserve noted that merchants could be negatively affected if large issuers were able to persuade their customers to pay with credit cards rather than debit cards, since credit cards generally have higher interchange fees.[147] While issuers can take this strategy, merchants also can provide incentives to consumers to encourage them to use debit cards instead of credit cards. The Dodd-Frank Act requires networks to allow merchants to offer discounts to consumers based on whether they pay by cash, check, debit card, or credit card.[148] In addition, a recent report stated that an antitrust settlement between the Department of Justice and VISA and MasterCard requires the networks to loosen past restrictions on merchants' ability to offer discounts to consumers based on the payment method, brand, and product. This allows merchants accepting cards by those networks to provide incentives to encourage customers to complete their debit transactions using their PIN rather than signature.[149] GAO did not identify data on whether issuers or merchants are engaging in such strategies.

Some types of merchants may be adversely affected by Regulation II. As mentioned earlier, the fee cap generally led payment card networks to set their debit interchange fees at the level of the cap for covered issuers. However, the interchange fee for small-ticket transactions, or transactions that are generally under $15, was sometimes below the fee cap before Regulation II became effective. For example, according to the International Franchise Association and the National Council of Chain Restaurants, before Regulation II a $5 transaction could incur 11.75 cents in debit interchange fees.[150] Under the current fee cap of 21 cents plus 0.05 percent of the transaction value, the interchange fee for a $5 covered transaction is 21.25 cents, about 80 percent higher. As a result, merchants that have a high volume of small value transactions, such as quick serving restaurants, transit authorities, and self-service and vending operators, could be worse off after the adoption of Regulation II.

It is not practical to measure the extent to which consumers in the many markets where debit transactions are possible have been affected by Regulation II.[151] First, one probable outcome is that at least a fraction of the merchants have passed some of their cost savings onto consumers. As noted by the Federal Reserve, whether merchants reduce their prices as a result of lower interchange fees will depend on the competitiveness of the various retail markets. In a competitive market with low margins, merchants likely have to pass on at least part of their cost savings to consumers. On the other hand, the loss in debit interchange fee income by large banks may lead them to seek ways to recover that lost income. As mentioned by the Federal Reserve, banks may try to recoup lost interchange fee income by introducing new bank service and product fees, possibly making banking services too costly for at least some customers. Our analysis (discussed previously) suggests that covered banks have recovered some of their lost interchange fee revenue, such as through increased revenue from service charges on deposit accounts.[152]

Impact on Competition and Interchange Fees

Historically, issuers have determined which and how many signature and PIN networks may process their debit card transactions. Before and after Regulation II, issuers generally use only one signature network (e.g., VISA or MasterCard) to process their debit card transactions that are completed using a signature. Additionally, as stated in the final rule, before Regulation II issuer banks, or in some cases, networks controlled the merchant routing of debit transactions. For example, an issuer bank could require a PIN transaction to be routed over a particular network, even if other PIN networks were available to route the transaction. The rule also states that, prior to Regulation II, issuer banks were able to limit the networks enabled on their cards through exclusive contracts with networks. For example, some issuers had agreed to restrict their cards' signature debit functionality to a single signature debit network and their PIN debit functionality to the signature network's affiliated PIN network. According to the Federal Reserve's 2009 survey data of large issuers, most debit cards from large bank issuers carried only one PIN network, and the cards' PIN and signature networks typically were affiliated with each other.[153]

Regulation II contains two provisions that serve to provide merchants with the option of selecting the network to process their debit card transactions and a greater number of network options. First, the rule prohibits all issuers and networks from inhibiting a merchant from directing the routing of a transaction over any network allowed by the issuer. This provision became effective on October 1, 2011. For example, if an issuer's debit card has two or more PIN networks, the merchant rather than the issuer can chose which network processes a PIN transaction, such as the one charging the lowest interchange fee. Second, the rule prohibits all issuers and networks from restricting the number of networks over which debit transactions may be processed to fewer than two unaffiliated networks. This provision became effective on April 1, 2012. As a result, issuers no longer may allow only VISA's or MasterCard's signature and affiliated PIN networks to process their debit card transactions. Instead, such issuers would need to add an unaffiliated signature or PIN network if they do not already have an unaffiliated network.[154]

Regulation II's prohibitions may have a limited impact on increasing competition and, in turn, lowering interchange fees, because issuers largely control which networks may process their debit card transactions. For example, issuers did not likely comply with Regulation II by adding a second unaffiliated signature network because, according to the final rule, networks and issuers stated it would be too costly to reconfigure cards and merchant equipment to enable the processing of two signature networks associated with one card.[155] Consequently, merchants generally have only one network option for transactions completed by signature. Additionally, issuers can comply by having an unaffiliated signature network and PIN network, which means that merchants may have only one network routing choice once a customer decides to use her signature or her PIN. Therefore, even though Regulation II provides merchants with the authority to choose the network over which to route debit card transactions, merchants may not have a choice about which network to route the debit card transaction.

Going forward, issuers may be able to act strategically to limit competition over debit card interchange fees through their control over which networks may process their debit card transactions. First, for covered transactions subject to the fee cap, both signature and PIN networks have an incentive to set their interchange fees at the fee cap.[156] If a network lowered its fees below the cap, such as to attract merchant routing business, issuers using that network could replace it with a network that sets its fees at the cap. With networks charging similar interchange fees for covered transactions, merchants may not be able to use their network routing decisions to put downward pressure on such fees. Second, for exempt PIN transactions, merchants may be able to exert downward pressure on fees when issuers use two or more PIN networks to process their transactions.[157] In this case, merchants can choose the network with the lowest fees and possibly induce the other networks to lower their fees. However, exempt issuers may be able to counter such pressure by dropping a network whose fees are too low or allowing only the PIN network (along with an unaffiliated signature network) with the highest fees to process their transactions. As discussed, merchants may be able to provide incentives to customers using cards issued by exempt banks to conduct a PIN rather than a signature transaction, so as to allow themselves more routing options.[158]

Impact on Networks

In response to Regulation II, VISA is undertaking strategies intended to attract merchant routing. First, VISA recently imposed a new monthly fixed acquirer fee that merchants must pay to accept VISA debit and credit cards. VISA also plans to reduce merchants' variable fees so that merchants' total fees associated with VISA transactions likely would be lower after the new fee structure's implementation.[159] Under its new fee structure, VISA could, for example, lower the interchange fees for VISA's PIN network, Interlink, to attract merchant routing and make up at least some of its lost revenue by collecting the fixed fees.[160]

However, the extent to which VISA will be able to lower PIN debit interchange fees and gain transaction volume is limited. As with any network, if Interlink reduces its interchange fees too much, issuers could replace Interlink with another PIN network that offers higher fees.

Second, according to VISA representatives, VISA's signature network also is able to process PIN transactions, in essence automatically offering an additional PIN routing choice to merchants for cards that carry VISA signature.[161] For example, in the past, a debit card that carried the VISA signature and two other PIN networks usually would process a PIN transaction through one of the PIN networks. Now, the VISA check card signature network can continue to be the only option for routing signature debit transactions on that card but also become a third option for routing PIN debit transactions.

For VISA to gain PIN transaction volume through VISA check cards, however, it must set the associated interchange fees at or below the fees set by the other available PIN networks. However, the extent to which VISA can do this is not yet clear. If issuers experienced declining interchange fee revenue from their use of VISA, they could switch signature networks, for example, to MasterCard.

APPENDIX VI. ECONOMETRIC ANALYSIS OF THE IMPACT THE DEBIT INTERCHANGE FEE STANDARD ON ISSUER BANKS' INCOME

Methodology

We conducted an econometric analysis to assess the impact of the Dodd-Frank Act's debit interchange fee standard on covered banks.[162] Our multivariate econometric model used a difference-in-difference design that exploits the fact that some banks are automatically covered by the debit interchange fee requirements but others are not, so we can view covered banks as the treatment group and exempt banks as the control group. We then compared changes in various types of income earned by covered banks over time to changes in those types of income earned by exempt banks over time. All else being equal, the difference in the differences is the impact of the new debit interchange fee requirements.

Our regression specification is the following:

$$y_{bq} = \alpha_b + \beta_q + \gamma_q COVERED_{bq} + X'_{bq}\Theta + \varepsilon_{bq},$$

where b denotes the bank, q denotes the quarter, y_{bq} is the dependent variable, α_b is an institution-specific intercept, β^q is a quarter-specific intercept, $COVERED_{bq}$ is an indicator variable that equals 1 if bank b is covered by the debit interchange standard in quarter q and 0 otherwise, X_{bq} is a list of other independent variables, and ε_{bq} is an error term. We estimate the parameters of the model using quarterly data for banks for the period from the first quarter of 2008 to the second quarter of 2012.

The parameters of interest are the γ_q, the coefficients on the covered bank indicators in the quarters after the treatment start date of the fourth quarter of 2011. The debit interchange standard was effective October 1, 2011, (the fourth quarter of 2011), so the covered bank indicator is equal to zero for all banks for all quarters from the first quarter of 2008 to the third quarter of 2011. For all quarters from the fourth quarter of 2011 to the second quarter of 2012, the covered bank indicator is equal to one for all covered banks and equal to zero for all exempt banks. Thus, for quarters from the fourth of 2011 to the second of 2012, all else being equal, the parameter γ_q measures the average difference in the dependent variable between covered and exempt banks in that quarter relative to the base quarter.

We used lists of covered institutions provided by the Federal Reserve to identify which banks in our sample are required to comply with debit card interchange fee standards in each quarter and which are not. We assumed that any institution not explicitly identified as a covered institution was exempt.

We used different dependent variables (y_{bq}) in order to estimate the impacts of the debit interchange standard on various sources of income earned by covered banks, including

- bank card and credit card interchange fees,
- service charges on deposit accounts in domestic offices,
- total non-interest income,
- total interest income, and
- total income.

Finally, we included size as an independent variable (X_{bq}) to control for factors correlated with size that may differentially affect exempt and covered banks in the quarters since debit interchange standard went into effect. We measured the size of a bank as the natural logarithm of its total assets. We included this variable to reduce the likelihood that our estimates of the impact of the debit interchange standard are reflecting something else.

Data

To assess the impact of debit interchange fee regulation on covered institutions, we analyzed commercial banks and savings banks (banks) for the period from the first quarter of 2008 to the second quarter of 2012 using data from the Federal Reserve, the Federal Deposit Insurance Corporation (FDIC), and the Federal Financial Institutions Examination Council (FFIEC). We excluded savings associations and credit unions from our analysis, even though they are subject to the debit card interchange fee standards. For much of the period we analyzed, savings associations filed quarterly Thrift Financial Reports, but these filings did not include the information we required for our analysis, such as income earned from bank card and credit card interchange fees, for every quarter. Similarly, credit union filings also do not include the information we required for our analysis.

RESULTS

Table 14 shows the estimated differences in fees and income as a percent of assets for covered banks relative to what they would have earned in the absence of the debit interchange fee standard, all else being equal.

Our estimates suggest that the debit interchange fee standard is associated with:

- *Lower bank card and credit card interchange fees collected by covered banks.* After the effective date, interchange fees collected by covered banks, as a percent of assets, were about 0.007-0.008 percentage points lower than they otherwise would have been. For a bank with assets of $50 billion, this amounts to $3.5 million-4 million in reduced bank card and credit card interchange fees.
- *Higher service charges on deposit accounts in domestic offices for covered banks.* After the effective date, service charges collected by covered banks, as a percent of assets, were about 0.004-0.007 percentage points higher than they otherwise would have been. For a bank with assets of $50 billion, this amounts to $2 million-3.5 million in additional service charges.
- *No significant change in overall non-interest income for covered banks.* Non-interest income—of which both interchange fees and service charges are components—earned by covered banks was about 0.09-0.13 percentage points lower as a percent of assets than it would have been in the first two quarters after the effective date and about 0.03 percentage points higher in the third quarter after the effective date. However, these estimates are not statistically significant at the 5-percent level.
- *Increased interest income in the first two quarters after the effective date but no significant increase since.* Interest income earned by covered banks, as a percent of assets, was about 0.03 percentage points higher than it would have been in the first two quarters after the effective date. It was 0.02 percentage points higher in the third quarter after the effective date, but this estimate is not statistically significant at the 5-percent level.
- *No significant change in total income.* Total income—which is composed of interest and non-interest income—earned by covered banks after the effective date, as a percent of assets, ranges from 0.10

percentage points lower to 0.05 percentage points higher, but these estimates are not statistically significant at the 5-percent level.

Table 14. Estimated Impact of the Debit Interchange Fee Standard on Covered Banks, from Fourth Quarter of 2011 through Second Quarter of 2012 (percentage points)

Covered in:	Bank card and credit card interchange fees (% of assets)	Service charges on deposit accounts in domestic offices (% of assets)	Non-interest income (% of assets)	Interest income (% of assets)	Total income (% of assets)
2011 Q4	-0.007**	0.004**	-0.094	0.027**	-0.074
	(0.001)	(0.001)	(0.085)	(0.014)	(0.086)
2012 Q1	-0.007**	0.007**	-0.125	0.026**	-0.101
	(0.001)	(0.001)	(0.073)	(0.013)	(0.074)
2012 Q2	-0.008**	0.007**	0.029	0.022	0.049
	(0.001)	(0.002)	(0.089)	(0.014)	(0.090)
Observations	128,059	128,059	128,059	128,059	128,059
Within R-squared	0.054	0.196	0.003	0.608	0.171
Number of banks	7,815	7,815	7,815	7,815	7,815
All impacts jointly significant?	Yes	Yes	No	No	No

Source: GAO analysis of data from FDIC, FFIEC, and the Federal Reserve.

Note: Estimated impacts are of the debit fee standard on (1) bank card and credit card interchange fees, (2) service charges on deposit accounts in domestic offices, (3) noninterest income, (4) interest income, and (5) total income, as a percent of assets, for covered banks after the effective date of the debit interchange regulation. Robust standard errors are in parentheses. We obtained the estimates using regressions of bank card and credit card interchange fees, service charges on deposit accounts in domestic offices, noninterest income, interest income, and total income, as a percent of assets, on the natural logarithm of assets, indicators for each bank, indicators for each quarter, and indicators for covered banks in each quarter after the effective date of the debit interchange regulation. We used F-tests to determine whether the indicators for covered banks in each quarter are jointly significant. We used t-tests to determine whether the indicators for covered banks in each quarter are individually significant. We used the 5 percent level as our criteria for statistical significance. **=statistically significant at the 5 percent level.

To assess the robustness of our estimates, we examined different treatment start dates. Specifically, we allowed the debit fee standard to have an impact starting in the fourth quarter of 2010—1 year prior to the rule's effective date—on banks that were covered in the fourth quarter of 2011. We did so to allow for the possibility that institutions began to react to the debit fee standard in anticipation of the rule being passed. Our estimates suggest that changes in covered banks' interchange fee income and service charge income generally did not occur until after the effective date and also that significant changes in non-interest income, interest income, and total income for covered banks generally did not precede the rule's effective date.

Our approach allows us to partially differentiate changes in various types of income earned by covered banks associated with the debit interchange fee cap from changes due to other factors. However, several factors make isolating and measuring the impact of the cap for covered banks challenging. In particular, the effects of the cap cannot be differentiated from simultaneous changes in economic conditions, regulations, or other changes that may differentially affect covered banks. Nevertheless, our estimates are suggestive of the initial effects of the cap on covered banks and provide a baseline against which to compare future trends.

End Notes

[1] Pub. L. No. 111-203, 124 Stat. 1376 (2010).

[2] Exec. Order No. 12,866, 58 Fed. Reg. 51,735 (Sept. 30, 1993), as supplemented and reaffirmed by Exec. Order No. 13,563, 76 Fed. Reg. 3821 (Jan. 21, 2011).

[3] Independent regulatory agencies are those defined by 44 U.S.C. § 3502(5).

[4] Pub. L. No. 112-10, § 1573(a), 125 Stat. 38, 138-39 (2011) (codified at 12 U.S.C. § 5496b). Under the mandate, we are directed to analyze (1) the impact of regulation on the financial marketplace, including the effects on the safety and soundness of regulated entities, cost and availability of credit, savings realized by consumers, reductions in consumer paperwork burden, changes in personal and small business bankruptcy filings, and costs of compliance with rules, including whether relevant federal agencies are applying sound cost-benefit analysis in promulgating rules; (2) efforts to avoid duplicative or conflicting rulemakings, information requests, and examinations; and (3) other matters deemed appropriate by the Comptroller General. As agreed with congressional staff, the focus of our reviews will be limited to the financial regulations promulgated pursuant to the Dodd-Frank Act.

[5] GAO, *Dodd-Frank Act Regulations: Implementation Could Benefit from Additional Analyses and Coordination*, GAO-12-151 (Washington, D.C.: Nov. 10, 2011).

[6] In this report, we use the term rules generally to refer to Federal Register notices of agency action pursuant to the Dodd-Frank Act, including regulations, interpretive rules, general statements of policy, and rules that deal with agency organization, procedure, or practice.

[7] A complete list of all Dodd-Frank Act rules in effect as of July 23, 2012, can be found in appendix II.

[8] 5 U.S.C. § 553.

[9] As defined by the Congressional Review Act, a major rule is a rule that the Administrator of the Office of Information and Regulatory Affairs within OMB finds has resulted in or is likely

to result in (1) an annual effect on the economy of $100 million or more, (2) a major increase in costs or prices, or (3) significant adverse effects on competition, employment, investment, productivity, or innovation. 5 U.S.C. § 804(2). This is similar, but not identical, to the definition of a "significant regulatory action" under E.O. 12866.

[10] As independent regulatory agencies that are not required to follow the economic analysis requirements of E.O. 12,866, the financial regulators also are not required to follow OMB Circular A-4. However, Circular A-4 is an example of best practices for agencies to follow when conducting regulatory analyses, and the financial regulators have told us that they follow the guidance in principle or spirit.

[11] The Dodd-Frank Act does not use the term "systemically important financial institution" (SIFI). This term is commonly used by academics and other experts to refer to bank holding companies with $50 billion or more in total consolidated assets and nonbank financial companies designated by FSOC for Federal Reserve supervision and enhanced prudential standards under the Dodd-Frank Act. For purposes of this report, we refer to these bank and nonbank financial companies as bank systemically important financial institutions (bank SIFI) and nonbank systemically important financial institutions (nonbank SIFI), respectively. We also refer to nonbank SIFIs and bank SIFIs collectively as SIFIs when appropriate.

[12] 12 U.S.C. § 5581.

[13] The provisions of the Dodd-Frank Act concerning FSOC are contained primarily in subtitle A of title I, §§ 111-123, codified at 12 U.S.C. §§ 5321-5333, and title VIII, codified at 12 U.S.C. §§ 5461-5472.

[14] The 10 voting members provide a federal regulatory perspective and an independent insurance expert's view. The 5 nonvoting members offer different insights as state-level representatives from bank, securities, and insurance regulators or as the directors of two new offices within Treasury—the Office of Financial Research and Federal Insurance Office—that were established by the Dodd-Frank Act. For additional information on FSOC, see GAO, Financial Stability: New Council and Research Office Should Strengthen the Accountability and Transparency of Their Decisions, GAO-12-886 (Washington, D.C.: Sept. 11, 2012).

[15] APA also contains requirements for formal rulemaking, which is used in rate-making proceedings and other cases involving a statute that requires rules to be made "on the record." Formal rulemaking incorporates evidentiary (or "trial type") hearings, in which interested parties may present evidence, conduct cross-examinations of other witnesses, and submit rebuttal evidence. However, few statutes require such on-the-record hearings.

[16] 5 U.S.C. § 553. The notice of proposed rulemaking is to contain (1) a statement of the time, place, and nature of public rulemaking proceedings; (2) reference to the legal authority under which the rule is proposed; and (3) either the terms or substance of the proposed rule or a description of the subjects and issues involved.

[17] 77 Fed. Reg. 30,596 (May 23, 2012).

[18] 77 Fed. Reg. 21,637 (Apr. 11, 2012).

[19] Pub. L. No. 104-13, 109 Stat. 163 (1995) (codified at 44 U.S.C. §§ 3501-3520); Pub. L. No. 96-354, 94 Stat. 1164 (1980) (codified at 5 U.S.C. §§ 601-612). PRA requires agencies to justify any collection of information from the public to minimize the paperwork burden the collection imposes and to maximize the practical utility of the information collected. 44 U.S.C. § 3504. RFA requires federal agencies to (1) assess the impact of their regulation on small entities, including businesses, governmental jurisdictions, and certain not-for-profit organizations with characteristics set forth in the act, and (2) consider regulatory alternatives to lessen the regulatory burden on small entities. 5 U.S.C. § 603.

[20] § 15(a), 42 Stat. 998 (1922) (codified, as amended, at 7 U.S.C. § 19(a).

[21] 12 U.S.C. § 5481(6).

[22] 5 U.S.C. §§ 603(d).

[23] Pub. L. No. 104-290, § 106(a), 110 Stat. 3416, 3424 (1996) (codified at 15 U.S.C. § 77b(b)). Conforming amendments to the Investment Advisers Act of 1940 were made in section 224 of the Gramm Leach Bliley Act. Pub. L. No. 106-102, § 224, 113 Stat. 1338, 1402 (1999) (codified at 15 U.S.C. § 80b-2(c)).

[24] § 23(a)(2), 48 Stat. 881 (1934) (codified at 15 U.S.C. § 78w(a)(2)).

[25] 15 U.S.C. § 1693b(a)(2).

[26] Exec. Order No. 12,866, 58 Fed. Reg. 51,735 (Sept. 30, 1993). For significant rules (those with an annual effect on the economy of $100 million or more, or that trigger one of the other specified criteria), the order further requires agencies to prepare a detailed regulatory (or economic) analysis of both the benefits and costs. More recently, E.O. 13,563 supplemented E.O. 12866, in part by incorporating its principles, structures, and definitions. Exec. Order No. 13,563, 76 Fed. Reg. 3,821 (Jan. 18, 2011). E.O. 12,866 contains 12 principles of regulation that direct agencies to perform specific analyses to identify the problem to be addressed, assess its significance, assess both the benefits and costs of the intended regulation, design the regulation in the most cost-effective manner to achieve the regulatory objective, and base decisions on the best reasonably obtained information available.

[27] OMB, Circular A-4: Regulatory Analysis, September 17, 2003. Circular A-4 refined OMB's "best practices" guidance issued in 1996 and 2000. Executive Order 13,579 (E.O. 13,579) encourages independent regulatory agencies to comply with E.O. 13563. Exec. Order No. 13,579, 76 Fed. Reg. 41,587 (July 14, 2011).

[28] Independent regulatory agencies are those defined by 44 U.S.C. § 3502(5). This statutory definition was revised by the Dodd-Frank Act to include OCC and other agencies.

[29] CFPB issued three rules that came into effect during our scope period, but none of the rules required public notice-and-comment rulemaking under APA.

[30] The agencies assess whether a rule is major using criteria in the Congressional Review Act and submit their assessment for determination by OMB. As defined by the Congressional Review Act, a major rule is a rule that OMB's Office of Information and Regulatory Affairs finds has resulted in or is likely to result in (1) an annual effect on the economy of $100 million or more; (2) a major increase in costs or prices; or (3) significant adverse effects on competition, employment, investment, productivity, or innovation. 5 U.S.C. § 804(2). This is similar, but not identical, to the definition of "significant regulatory action" under E.O. 12866.

[31] 77 Fed. Reg. 29,884 (May 21, 2012).

[32] See GAO

[33] E.O. 12,866 requires that covered federal agencies assess the benefits and costs of potentially effective and reasonably feasible alternatives to the planned regulation, identified by the agencies or the public. See Exec. Order No. 12,866, Section 6(a)(3)(C)(iii). In addition, Circular A-4 states that covered federal agencies should carefully consider all appropriate alternatives for the key attributes or provisions of the rule. See Circular No. A-4, at 16.

[34] CFTC's real-time publication rule was promulgated early in the Dodd-Frank Act implementation process, and CFTC staff stated that they have since made improvements to their economic analyses. SEC has since revised its guidance for economic analysis to include evaluation of the benefits and costs of alternative approaches, as discussed below.

[35] See http://www.federalreserve.gov/newsevents/press/bcreg/20110629a.htm (accessed Oct. 9, 2012) for the survey results and other releases related to the debit card interchange fee rule.

[36] 77 Fed. Reg. 1182, 1234.

[37] 77 Fed. Reg. 1182, 1232, 1233.

[38] 76 Fed. Reg. 34,300, 34,356. The four objectives were (i) encourage high quality submissions and discourage frivolous submissions; (ii) encourage whistleblowers to provide information early, rather than waiting to receive a request or inquiry from a relevant authority; (iii) minimize unnecessary burdens on whistleblowers and establish fair, transparent procedures; and (iv) promote the use of effective internal compliance programs in appropriate circumstances.

[39] Treasury, as noted above, is subject to E.O. 12,866 and Circular A-4.

[40] CFTC has separate guidance for proposed rules and final rules, issued in September 2010 and May 2011, respectively.

[41] SEC's guidance on economic analysis is available on the SEC website: http://www.sec.gov/divisions/riskfin.shtml.

[42] Pub. L. No. 111-203, § 171 (codified at 12 U.S.C. § 5371). The final rule promulgated under § 171 can be found at 76 Fed. Reg. 37,620 (June 28, 2011).

[43] Section 619 of the Dodd-Frank Act prohibits banking entities, including insured depository institutions (other than certain limited purpose trust companies), and their affiliates, which benefit from federal insurance on customer deposits or access to the discount window, from engaging in proprietary trading or investing in or sponsoring hedge funds or private equity funds, subject to certain exceptions. 12 U.S.C. § 1851.

[44] *The Annual Report of the Financial Stability Oversight Council*, Before the Committee on Financial Services, 112th Cong. 5 (Oct. 6, 2011) (statement of Timothy F. Geithner, Secretary of the Treasury).

[45] See GAO

[46] 76 Fed. Reg. 41,626, 41,628 (July 15, 2011).

[47] We primarily relied on *Federal Register* notices to determine whether coordination took place for the rules we reviewed, as the rule releases are supposed to contain the key steps agencies took to formulate the rules. Therefore, rules that may have involved interagency coordination but did not mention coordination in the *Federal Register* notices are not included in this table. For example, CFTC and SEC issued similar whistleblower protection rules; however, only CFTC mentioned interagency coordination in the rule release. SEC told us that they had consulted with CFTC on this rulemaking, but did not include a discussion of consultation in their rule release because CFTC's rule had not yet been issued. Therefore, only the CFTC rule is included in this table.

[48] Risk retention rulemaking is being conducted by FDIC, OCC, the Federal Reserve, SEC, the U.S. Department of Housing and Urban Development, and the Federal Housing Finance Agency, as required by section 941 of the Dodd-Frank Act, but has not yet been finalized. Pub. L. No. 111-203, § 941, 124 Stat. 1890 (2010) (codified at 15 U.S.C. § 78o-11).

[49] Swap data repositories are new entities created by the Dodd-Frank Act in order to provide a central facility for swap data reporting and recordkeeping. Under the act, all swaps, whether cleared or uncleared, are required to be reported to registered swap data repositories. Pub. L. No. 111-203, § 727, 124 Stat. 1696 (2010) (codified at 7 U.S.C. 2(a)(13)(G)).

[50] See GAO

[51] The seven agencies that did not have written policies and procedures were CFPB, CFTC, the Federal Reserve, FSOC, NCUA, OFR, and SEC. However, in our November 2011 report we noted that SEC and CFTC have a memorandum of understanding that establishes a permanent regulatory liaison between them and contains procedures to facilitate the discussion and coordination of regulatory action on issues of common regulatory interest.

[52] See GAO

[53] For example, the law firm Davis Polk & Wardwell LLP estimates that federal agencies will need to issue 398 rules to implement the Dodd-Frank Act but found the agencies had finalized 127 of the rules, or nearly 32 percent, as of October 1, 2012.

[54] See GAO

[55] The Dodd-Frank Act does not use the term "systemically important financial institution" (SIFI). This term is commonly used by academics and other experts to refer to bank holding companies with $50 billion or more in total consolidated assets and nonbank financial companies designated by FSOC for Federal Reserve supervision and enhanced prudential standards under the Dodd-Frank Act. For purposes of this report, we refer to these bank and nonbank financial companies as bank systemically important financial institutions (bank SIFI) and nonbank systemically important financial institutions (nonbank SIFI), respectively, or collectively as SIFIs.

[56] S. REP. No. 111-176 (2010).

[57] S. REP. No. 111-176 (2010).

[58] See appendix III for the rulemaking status and summary of SIFI-related provisions included in this section.

[59] We developed indicators for size, complexity, leverage, and liquidity of SIFIs. However, we did not develop indicators for interconnectedness in this report, but plan to do so in future reports as we and others learn more about potential ways that financial instability can spread across the financial system.

[60] As of October 31, 2012, FSOC had issued a final rule and interpretative guidance on the methodology it is using to designate nonbank financial companies for enhanced regulation and supervision by the Federal Reserve. According to Treasury officials, a number of firms are actively being considered pursuant to the designation process as described in those documents. Officials noted that at meetings on September 28 and October 18, 2012, FSOC voted to approve the advancement of initial subsets of nonbank financial companies to Stage 3, the final stage of evaluation before a proposed determination of designation is considered.

[61] Our analyses of bank SIFIs include U.S. bank holding companies with total consolidated assets of $50 billion or more and foreign bank organizations' U.S.-based bank holding company subsidiaries that on their own have total consolidated assets of $50 billion or more. The Federal Reserve's proposed regulations on enhanced prudential standards do not apply to foreign banking organizations, and the Federal Reserve expects to issue a separate proposal that would apply the enhanced standards of sections 165 and 166 of the act to foreign banking organizations. 77 Fed. Reg. 594 (Jan. 5, 2012).

[62] The Basel Committee has agreed on a new set of risk-based capital, leverage, liquidity, and other requirements for banking institutions (Basel III requirements). Additionally, the Financial Stability Board and the Basel Committee have agreed on new capital and other requirements applicable to designated globally systemically important banks (G-SIB requirements). U.S. banking regulators are in the process of implementing these requirements.

[63] Ben S. Bernanke, "Financial Reform to Address Systemic Risk," (Speech to the Council on Foreign Relations, Washington, D.C., Mar. 10, 2009).

[64] See, for example, Chairperson of the FSOC, Study of the Effects of Size and Complexity of Financial Institutions on Capital Market Efficiency and Economic Growth Pursuant to Section 123 of the Dodd-Frank Wall Street Reform and Consumer Protection Act of 2010 (Washington, D.C.: January 2011).

[65] In figure 1, bank SIFIs are bank holding companies with $50 billion or more in total consolidated assets as of the second quarter of 2012. Figure 1 shows assets for these bank SIFIs as of the third quarter of 2010 and the second quarter of 2012.

[66] FSOC, 2011 *Annual Report* (Washington D.C.: July, 2011), and FSOC, 2012 *Annual Report*, (Washington, D.C.: July, 2012).

[67] Pub. L. No. 111-203, § 165 (codified at 12 U.S.C. § 5365). The Federal Reserve and FDIC's final rule requiring resolution plans can be found at 76 Fed. Reg. 67,323 (Nov. 1, 2011). Additionally, FDIC issued a related final rule requiring resolution plans from insured depository institutions with $50 billion or more in total assets. While this rule does not implement a Dodd-Frank provision, FDIC intends to use these plans to evaluate potential loss severity at these institutions and enable the agency to perform its resolution functions most efficiently. 77 Fed. Reg. 3075 (Jan. 23, 2012).

[68] If the regulators find a SIFI's resolution plan to be deficient, they may place restrictions on the growth, activities, or operations of the SIFI and ultimately require the SIFI to divest certain assets or operations to facilitate an orderly resolution.

[69] Treasury's Office of Financial Research (OFR) is required to develop and maintain metrics and reporting systems for risks to financial stability. 12 U.S.C. § 5344(c)(1)(A). OFR has begun

to catalogue and analyze these measures. See Office of Financial Research, *2012 Annual Report* (Washington, D.C.: July 2012).

[70] G-SIBs are banks considered by the Financial Stability Board (FSB) to be of such size, market importance, and global interconnectedness that their distress or failure would cause significant dislocation in the global financial system and adverse economic consequences across a range of countries. FSB was established in April 2009 to coordinate at the international level the work of national financial authorities and international standard setting bodies and to develop and promote the implementation of effective regulatory, supervisory and other financial sector policies in the interest of financial stability. In 2010, FSB proposed a policy framework for addressing the systemic and moral hazard risks associated with global SIFIs, which includes requirements for resolution planning and additional loss absorption (i.e., capital surcharges) for global SIFIs.

[71] In November 2011, FSB identified 29 G-SIBs and indicated it would update this list annually each November. FSB updated this list on November 1, 2012. The updated list contains 28 G-SIBs; the same eight U.S. bank SIFIs were designated as G-SIBs in 2011 and 2012. Additionally, on November 1, 2012, FSB allocated each G-SIB into a bucket corresponding to its different levels of capital surcharge. FSB has not yet identified any nonbank G-SIFIs.

[72] As mentioned earlier, the Basel Committee has agreed on a new set of risk-based capital, leverage, liquidity, and other requirements for banking institutions (Basel III requirements). Additionally, the Financial Stability Board and the Basel Committee have agreed on new capital and other requirements applicable to designated globally systemically important banks (G-SIB requirements). U.S. banking regulators are in the process of implementing these requirements.

[73] For example, some of the proposed Basel III reforms are expected to impose tighter or, in some cases, new capital and leverage requirements on U.S. banking institutions.

[74] 77 Fed. Reg. 594 (Jan. 5, 2012). The proposed regulations require all SIFIs to comply with any regulations adopted by the Federal Reserve relating to capital plans and stress tests. The proposal would apply existing capital plan requirements for large bank holding companies to nonbank SIFIs. Final regulations adopted by the Federal Reserve require banks with more than $50 billion in total assets to develop and submit annual capital plans. 12 C.F.R. § 225.8.

[75] 77 Fed. Reg. 594 (Jan. 5, 2012). Also see, Basel Committee on Banking Supervision, *Global Systemically Important Banks: Assessment Methodology and the Additional Loss Absorbency Requirement* (Basel, Switzerland, November 2011).

[76] Tangible common equity subtracts intangible assets, goodwill, and preferred stock equity from a company's total equity. Risk-weighted assets are on- and off-balance sheet assets adjusted for certain characteristics that may be associated with risk.

[77] As mentioned earlier, the Basel Committee has agreed on a new set of risk-based capital, leverage, liquidity, and other requirements for banking institutions (Basel III requirements). Additionally, the Financial Stability Board and the Basel Committee have agreed on new capital and other requirements applicable to designated globally systemically important banks (G-SIB requirements). U.S. banking regulators are in the process of implementing these requirements.

[78] 77 Fed. Reg. 594 (Jan. 5, 2012). Liquidity risk management standards would, among other things, require a SIFI to project cash flow needs over various time horizons, stress test the projections at least monthly, and maintain a contingency funding plan that identifies potential sources of liquidity strain and alternative sources of funding. The size of the required liquidity buffer is based on cash flow projections and liquidity stress testing and would require a SIFI to continuously maintain a liquidity buffer sufficient to meet projected net cash outflows for 30 days over a range of liquidity stress scenarios.

[79] 77 Fed. Reg. 594 (Jan. 5, 2012). The Basel III liquidity requirements include the liquidity coverage ratio and the net stable funding ratio. The liquidity coverage ratio would impose a liquidity buffer to meet expected 30-day net cash outflows under various stress scenarios.

The net stable funding ratio would establish a floor for stable funding over a 1 year horizon to ensure that long-term assets are funded with at least a minimum amount of stable liabilities. See Basel Committee on Banking Supervision, *Basel III: International Framework for Liquidity Risk Measurement, Standards, and Monitoring* (Basel, Switzerland, December 2010).

[80] We measure short-term liabilities as the sum of federal funds purchased and repurchase agreements, trading liabilities (less derivatives with negative fair value), other borrowed funds, deposits held in foreign offices, and large time deposits held in domestic offices, where large time deposits are defined as time deposits greater than $100,000 prior to March 2010 and as time deposits greater than $250,000 in and after March 2010. We measure liquid assets as the sum of cash and balances due from depository institutions, securities (less pledged securities), federal funds sold and reverse repurchases, and trading assets.

[81] Because these limitations affect both the numerator and the denominator of our indicators, we cannot determine whether the exclusion of off-balance sheet items results in an under- or an overstatement of an institution's liquidity need and access.

[82] See appendix IV for more information on our econometric analysis.

[83] See, for example, Basel Committee on Banking Supervision, *An Assessment of the Long Term Economic Impact of Stronger Capital and Liquidity Requirements* (Basel, Switzerland, August 2010), and Basel Committee on Banking Supervision and Financial Stability Board, Assessing the *Macroeconomic Impact of the Transition to Stronger Capital and Liquidity Requirements* (Basel, Switzerland, August 2010). In a forthcoming report, we broadly discuss potential benefits and costs of the Dodd-Frank Act, including provisions related to stricter capital and leverage requirements.

[84] For more information on these and other provisions affecting SIFIs see appendix III.

[85] 77 Fed. Reg. 594 (Jan. 5, 2012).

[86] Bank SIFIs are currently required to comply with some of the enhanced prudential standards proposed on January 5, 2012 by the Federal Reserve. For example, the January 5, 2012 proposal would have nonbank financial companies designated by FSOC for Federal Reserve supervision be subject to the Federal Reserve's capital plan rule, which became effective for bank SIFIs on December 30, 2011. 76 Fed. Reg. 74,631 (Dec. 1, 2011). Additionally, on November 1, 2011, the Federal Reserve and FDIC finalized a rule implementing section 165(d) of the act which requires resolution plans from bank holding companies with $50 billion or more in total assets and nonbank financial companies designated by FSOC for Federal Reserve supervision. 76 Fed. Reg. 67,323 (Nov. 1, 2011). Bank SIFIs with $250 billion or more in total nonbank assets were required to submit these plans on July 1, 2012. See appendix III for more information on the status of the enhanced prudential standards required under the Dodd-Frank Act.

[87] 77 Fed. Reg. 594 (Jan. 5, 2012).

[88] We analyzed four rules that were final as of July 21, 2011. See appendix I for more details on our rule selection.

[89] As defined by the Congressional Review Act, a major rule is a rule that the Administrator of the Office of Information and Regulatory Affairs within OMB finds has resulted in or is likely to result in (1) an annual effect on the economy of $100 million or more; (2) a major increase in costs or prices; or (3) significant adverse effects on competition, employment, investment, productivity, or innovation. 5 U.S.C. § 804(2).

[90] 76 Fed. Reg. 43,394 (Jul. 20, 2011).

[91] 77 Fed. Reg. 46,258 (Aug. 3. 2012). EFTA Section 920 permits the Federal Reserve to allow for an adjustment to an interchange transaction fee that is reasonably necessary to make allowance for costs incurred by the issuer in preventing fraud in relation to electronic debit transactions, provided the issuer complies with standards established by the Federal Reserve relating to fraud prevention.

[92] The parties involved in an electronic debit card transaction are (1) the customer, or debit cardholder, (2) the bank that issued the debit card to the customer (issuer bank); (3) the

merchant; (4) the merchant's bank (called the acquirer bank), and (5) the payment card network that processes the transaction between the merchant acquirer bank and the issuer bank. In a debit transaction, the merchant receives the amount of the purchase minus a fee that it must pay to its acquirer bank. This fee includes the debit interchange fee that the acquirer bank pays to the issuer.

[93] See GAOfor a discussion of the rule's impact on small issuers.

[94] The Federal Reserve published data on interchange fees for 16 card networks from January 1, 2011 to December 31, 2011. According to Federal Reserve staff, totals published include data from 2 additional networks.

[95] See appendix VI for a more detailed discussion of our regression analysis.

[96] Our regression analysis suggests that covered banks have recovered some of their lost interchange fee revenue, such as through increased revenue from service charges on deposit accounts. See appendix VI for more details on our regression analysis.

[97] Competition in the supply of acquirer services is expected to cause acquirer banks to adjust the fees they charge to merchants and pass on any savings to avoid losing merchant business.

[98] Interchange fees generally combine an ad-valorem component, which depends on the amount of the transaction, and a fixed-fee component. Before Regulation II was implemented, fees more widely varied based on, among other things, the type of merchant. In some cases, the interchange fee for small-ticket transactions, or transactions that are generally under $15, were below the fee cap before Regulation II became effective. Since then, payment card networks have generally set their interchange fees at the level of the cap for covered issuers, so interchange fees for small-ticket transactions using cards issued by covered issuers have likely increased.

[99] EFTA section 920 also requires the Federal Reserve to prescribe rules that prohibit issuers and payment card networks from restricting the number of networks on which an electronic debit transaction may be processed to one such network or two or more networks operated by affiliated persons.

[100] EFTA section 920 also requires the Federal Reserve to prescribe rules prohibiting issuers and networks from inhibiting the ability of any person that accepts debit cards from directing the routing of electronic debit transactions over any network that may process such transactions.

[101] Consumers authenticate and complete electronic debit card transactions by entering a personal identification number (PIN) or their signature. In its rule proposal, the Federal Reserve considered requiring issuers to allow at least two unaffiliated signature networks and two unaffiliated PIN networks to process their debit card transactions. However, according to the final rule, networks and issuers stated it would be too costly to reconfigure cards and merchant equipment to enable the processing of two signature networks associated with one card. 75 Fed. Reg. 81,722 (Dec. 28, 2010).

[102] VISA representatives have explained publicly that this new fee structure is a strategic response to Regulation II. They said that VISA's PIN network, Interlink, lost significant transaction volume due to Regulation II, and the new fee structure is one of the company's strategies to regain some of the lost market share. VISA representatives stated that on March 13, 2012, the Department of Justice Antitrust Division issued a civil investigative demand requesting additional information about the company's debit strategies, including this fixed acquirer fee.

[103] Representatives from VISA said this move was a strategic response to their loss of market share associated with Regulation II. VISA representatives stated that on March 13, 2012, the Department of Justice Antitrust Division issued a civil investigative demand requesting additional information about the company's debit strategies, including information about the VISA signature debit network's ability to authenticate PIN transactions.

[104] 76 Fed. Reg. 4231 (Jan. 25, 2011). The initial proposed rule also included "consideration of rules to implement Section 15E(s)(4)(A) of the Exchange Act, which requires issuers or underwriters of any asset-backed security to make publicly available the findings and

conclusions of any third-party due diligence report the issuer or underwriter obtains." 75 Fed. Reg. 64,182 (Oct. 19, 2010). The final adoption has been delayed based on the suggestion by several commentators that the new Exchange Act Section 15E(s)(4) should be read as a whole.

[105] 76 Fed. Reg. 4231 (Jan. 25, 2011). According to SEC staff, most ABS that comprise residential mortgage-backed securities are issued or guaranteed by a government sponsored agency, such as the Federal National Mortgage Association (Fannie Mae), the Federal Home Loan Mortgage Corporation (Freddie Mac), or the Government National Mortgage Association (Ginnie Mae), and are exempt from registration under the Securities Act and reporting under the Exchange act.

[106] 76 Fed. Reg. 4231 (Jan. 25, 2011).

[107] 76 Fed. Reg. 4489 (Jan. 26, 2011). According to SEC, ABS sponsors or originators typically make representations and warranties about the quality of the underlying assets in an ABS. If the assets do not comply with the representations or warranties, a sponsor usually must repurchase or replace the assets. For example, in the case of residential mortgage backed securities, one representation and warranty is that each of the loans has complied with applicable federal, state, and local laws, including truth-in-lending, consumer credit protection, laws that protect against predatory and abusive practices, and disclosure laws. Another representation is that no fraud has taken place in connection with the origination of the assets on the part of the originator or any party involved in the origination of the assets.

[108] According to the Securities Industry and Financial Markets Association (SIFMA), agency mortgage-related ABS include Ginnie Mae, Fannie Mae, and Freddie Mac mortgage-backed securities and collateralized mortgage obligations (single and multifamily), as well as FDIC and NCUA structured transactions. The latter are backed by assets of failed banks and credit unions, respectively, and may include non-mortgage related collateral. Dollar amounts are adjusted for inflation and are expressed in constant 2012 Q2 dollars.

[109] Other ABS include home equity, auto, credit card, equipment, manufactured housing, student loan, non-agency mortgage-related, and other ABS.

[110] Dollar amounts are adjusted for inflation and are expressed in constant 2012 Q2 dollars.

[111] Section 951 requires disclosure of any agreements or understandings that the person making a proxy or consent solicitation has with named executive officers of the acquiring issuer concerning any type of compensation that is based on or relates to the acquisition, merger, consolidation, sale, or other disposition of all or substantially all of the assets of the issuer and the aggregate total of all such compensation that may be paid or become payable to or on behalf of such executive officer. 15 U.S.C. § 78n-1.

[112] 76 Fed. Reg. 6010 (Feb. 2, 2011).

[113] Section 951 provides that SEC may exempt an issuer from the advisory voting requirements. In determining whether to make an exemption, SEC is to take into account, among other considerations, whether the requirements disproportionately burden small issuers. A "smaller reporting company" is defined in rule 12b-2 under the Exchange Act, and includes companies that had a public float of less than $75 million as of the last business day of the issuer's most recently completed second fiscal quarter.

[114] A proxy season is the period of the year during which many companies hold their annual shareholder meetings, which is typically between March and June.

[115] A shareholder can choose to vote "for" or "against" a say-on-pay proposal. She can also choose to take a neutral stance and submit an "abstain" vote. If a shareholder fails to provide instructions to her broker, the corresponding votes are categorized as "broker non-votes." Institutional Shareholder Services (ISS) measured failed proposals as those where the "against" votes outnumber the "for" votes. According to market experts, some companies define failed proposals as those where more than 50 percent of the sum of "for," "against," and "abstain" votes are votes "against" the proposal.

[116] Russell 3000 companies are those included in the Russell 3000 Index, which comprises the largest 3,000 U.S. public companies and, according to Russell Investments, represents about 98 percent of the U.S. equity market.

[117] Although the percentage of failed votes was low in 2011, the report states that the actual number of failed votes was relatively high "compared with the track record of say on pay in other countries and the expectations of corporate government professionals." According to the report, shareholders defined the disconnect between pay and performance to mean that (1) the performance of a firm was below the peer group median (as measured by total absolute shareholder return (TSR) over 1, 3, or 5 years); or (2) absolute performance based on other financial measures. Council of Institutional Investors, *Say-On-Pay: Identifying Investor Concerns* (September 2011).

[118] A report from Semler Brossy, an executive compensation consulting firm, indicated that about 90 percent of firms have received at least 70 percent shareholder approval on say- on-pay proposals in 2011 and 2012. According to the report, 91 percent and 93 percent of companies received at least 70 percent of shareholder approval for their say-on-pay proposals in 2012 and 2011, respectively. See Semler Brossy, *2012 Say on Pay Results: Russell 3000 Shareholder Voting* (Sept. 5, 2012).

[119] According to ISS, as of September 1, 2011, annual votes received majority support at 80.1 percent of companies in the Russell 3000 index, as compared to triennial votes, which received majority support at 18.5 percent of companies. See *ISS, 2011 U.S. Postseason Report* (Sept. 29, 2011).

[120] Semler Brossy, *2012 Say on Pay Results: Russell 3000 Shareholder Voting* (Sept. 5, 2012). An earlier study by the firm stated that potential reasons behind the increase in shareholder say-on-pay approval from 2011 to 2012 included increased weighting of performance-based equity tied to specific performance measures in long-term incentive programs, significant shareholder outreach efforts, and a reduction in problematic pay practices. Semler Brossy, *Say on Pay Behind the Numbers: How Have Companies Responded to Failed 2011 Say on Pay Votes?* (May 18, 2012).

[121] Our analyses of bank SIFIs include U.S. bank holding companies with total consolidated assets of $50 billion or more and foreign bank organizations' U.S.-based bank holding company subsidiaries that on their own have total consolidated assets of $50 billion or more.

[122] SNL Financial reports data for bank holding companies based on forms FR Y-9C submitted to the Federal Reserve.

[123] The National Information Center is a central repository of data about banks and other institutions for which the Federal Reserve has a supervisory, regulatory, or research interest, including both domestic and foreign banking organizations operating in the United States.

[124] For this report, we did not develop indicators for interconnectedness, but expect to do so in the future.

[125] The cost of credit is determined by many factors other than bank SIFIs' cost of funding, including expected credit losses and administrative costs, as well as overall demand for credit and the availability of credit from other lenders.

[126] 76 Fed. Reg. 43,394 (Jul. 20, 2011).

[127] Debit interchange fees generally are the same for all issuing banks participating in a network. For example, all issuers that use VISA signature as their card network generally receive the same interchange fees set by VISA, although the fees can vary based on the type of transaction and whether the issuer bank is covered or exempt from the fee cap.

[128] For example, according to VISA's fee schedule as of October 2007, one interchange fee for a restaurant debit transaction was set at 1.19 percent of the transaction value plus $0.10.

[129] According to VISA's fee schedule as of October 2007, for example, a $20 debit transaction at a restaurant could cost about $0.34 (subject to an interchange fee of 1.19% + $0.10), while a $20 transaction at a car rental could cost about $0.42 (subject to an interchange fee of 1.36% + $0.15).

[130] See, for example, Marc Rysman, "The Economics of Two-Sided Markets," *Journal of Economic Perspectives*, vol. 23, no. 3, (summer 2009), pp. 125-143. In general, a two- sided market is one in which (1) two sets of agents interact through an intermediary or platform, and 2) the decisions of each set of agents affects the outcomes of the other set of agents, typically through an externality. In the case of debit cards, the intermediary is the network, and the two sets of agents are consumers and merchants. Neither consumers nor merchants will be interested in a network's debit card if the other party is not. A successful debit card requires both consumer usage and merchant acceptance, where both consumers and merchants value each other's participation.

[131] Debit cards are capable of processing a transaction over one or multiple networks. Consequently, when consumers present their debit cards to merchants to make purchases, it may be possible to complete a given transaction over several different debit card networks.

[132] Terri Bradford and Fumiko Hayashi, *Developments in Interchange Fees in the United States and Abroad*, Payments System Research Briefing, Federal Reserve Bank of Kansas City (April 2008).

[133] 76 Fed. Reg. 43,394 (July 20, 2011).

[134] 77 Fed. Reg. 46,258 (Aug. 3. 2012). EFTA section 920 permits the Federal Reserve to allow for an adjustment to an interchange transaction fee that is reasonably necessary to make allowance for costs incurred by the issuer in preventing fraud in relation to electronic debit transactions, provided the issuer complies with standards established by the Federal Reserve relating to fraud prevention.

[135] 76 Fed. Reg. 43,394 (July 20, 2012). EFTA section 920 also requires the Federal Reserve to prescribe rules that prohibit issuers and payment card networks from restricting the number of networks on which an electronic debit transaction may be processed to one such network or two or more affiliated networks.

[136] 76 Fed. Reg. 43, 394 (July 20, 2012). EFTA section 920 also requires the Federal Reserve to prescribe rules prohibiting issuers and networks from inhibiting the ability of any person that accepts debit cards from directing the routing of electronic debit transactions over any network that may process such transactions.

[137] These institutions were subject to the fee cap beginning July 1, 2012 because they had consolidated assets of $10 billion or more as of December 31, 2011.

[138] These institutions were exempt from the fee cap in 2012, because they had consolidated assets of less than $10 billion as of December 31, 2011. Institutions that qualified for the exemption during 2011 were those institutions that had, together with affiliates, assets of less than $10 billion as of December 31, 2010.

[139] The Federal Reserve published data on interchange fees for 16 card networks from January 1, 2011, to December 31, 2011. According to Federal Reserve staff, totals published include data from two additional networks.

[140] See appendix VI for details on our econometric analysis.

[141] GAO, *Community Banks and Credit Unions: Impact of the Dodd-Frank Act Depends Largely on Future Rulemakings*, GAO-12-881 (Washington, D.C.: Sept. 13, 2012). A two- tiered fee structure is one that offers different fee structures for exempt and covered issuers. For example, VISA USA Consumer Check Card fee schedule as of June 2012 set the interchange fee at the level of the cap for covered issuers, but kept the previous fee structure for exempt banks. That is, exempt banks continue to collect a wide variety of interchange fees determined by, among other things, the merchant type.

[142] As mentioned earlier, the Federal Reserve published data on interchange fees for 16 card networks from January 1, 2011, to December 31, 2011. According to Federal Reserve staff, totals published include data from two additional networks.

[143] The Federal Reserve published data from 16 payment card networks individually. Eight networks reported a decline in their average interchange fee per transaction for exempt issuers—ranging from $0.01 to $0.04—after the rule took effect. Three networks reported no change in their average interchange fee for exempt issuers. Five networks reported an

increase in their fee for exempt issuers—ranging from $0.01 to $0.03—after the rule took effect.

[144] The interchange fee as a percentage of the average transaction value is calculated by dividing the total interchange fees by the value of settled purchase transactions.

[145] A number of merchant associations have brought a lawsuit against the Federal Reserve, alleging that it failed to follow the intent of Congress regarding the amount of an interchange fee that an issuer could charge or receive. As of December 12, 2012, the suit had not been resolved.

[146] According to the Federal Reserve, merchant discount fees generally follow two forms: interchange-plus pricing and blended. If an acquirer is charging an interchange-plus merchant discount, the acquirer passes through the exact amount of the interchange fee for each transaction. If an acquirer is charging a blended merchant discount, the acquirer charges the same discount regardless of the interchange fee that applies to each transaction. Depending on the fee structure, it may take some time before an acquirer bank passes on savings from lower debit card interchange fees.

[147] For example, banks could try to eliminate debit card reward programs and offer relatively more attractive credit card rewards programs.

[148] EFTA Section 920(b)(2) prohibits a card network from establishing rules that prevent merchants from offering discounts or in-kind incentives based on the method of payment tendered to the extent that such discounts or incentives do not differentiate on the basis of the issuer or card network. According to a report by the Federal Reserve Bank of Kansas City, before the act, merchants were allowed by the Cash Discount Act to offer a discount to customers who pay with cash or check instead of credit cards, but networks did not allow merchants to offer a discount for paying with a debit card rather than a credit card. See Fumiko Hayashi, *Discounts and Surcharges: Implications for Consumer Payment Choice*, Payments System Research Briefing, Federal Reserve Bank of Kansas City (June 2012).

[149] Fumiko Hayashi, *Discounts and Surcharges: Implications for Consumer Payment Choice*, Payments System Research Briefing, Federal Reserve Bank of Kansas City (June 2012). According to the Federal Reserve, data collected from card networks in 2009 showed that the interchange fee per signature debit transaction was, on average, about 2.4 times that for a PIN debit transaction (2.6 times if calculated using the interchange fee as a percentage of the average transaction value).

[150] According to the International Franchise Association and National Council of Chain Restaurants, these would have been the resulting interchange fees under the VISA and MasterCard small-ticket transaction fees published about 7 months prior to the effective date of the fee cap, both set at 1.55 percent and 4 cents. See comments to the proposed rule by the International Franchise Association & National Council of Chain Restaurants available at http://www.federalreserve.gov/apps/foia/ViewAllComments.aspx?doc_id=R-1404&doc_ver=1.

[151] As the Federal Reserve indicated in its final rulemaking, it is not practical to measure the extent to which changes in interchange fees translate into changes in merchant prices because of the many other factors that also influence those prices.

[152] These service charges include amounts charged to depositors in domestic offices (1) for account maintenance, (2) for failure to maintain specified minimum deposit balances, (3) based on the number of checks drawn on and deposits made, (4) for checks drawn on so-called "no minimum balance" deposit accounts, (5) for withdrawals from nontransaction deposit accounts, (6) for the closing of savings accounts before a specified minimum period of time has elapsed, (7) for accounts which have remained inactive for extended periods of time or which have become dormant, (8) for deposits to or withdrawals from deposit accounts through the use of automated teller machines or remote service units, (9) for the processing of checks drawn against insufficient funds, (10) for issuing stop payment orders, (11) for certifying checks, and (12) for the accumulation or disbursement of funds deposited to Individual Retirement Accounts or Keogh Plan accounts when not handled by the bank's

trust department. Our analysis also suggests that covered issuer banks' total income has not changed significantly after Regulation II's fee cap became effective. Total income earned by covered banks, as a percent of assets, ranged from 0.10 percentage points lower to 0.05 percentage points higher after October 1, 2011, but these estimates are not statistically significant at the 5 percent level. See appendix VI for details of our econometric analysis.

[153] According to the survey, about 131.1 million out of 174.2 million debit cards that processed PIN transactions (or about 75 percent) carried only one PIN network. Additionally, about 105.5 million of the debit cards with one PIN network, or 80 percent, had a signature network that was affiliated with the PIN network. The final rule states that the Federal Reserve surveyed bank issuers that would be subject to the interchange fee standards (that is, banks with consolidated assets of $10 billion or more).

[154] Data from the Federal Reserve's survey of large issuer banks in 2009 showed that of almost 159 million of the banks' debit cards that carried both signature and PIN networks,105.5 million (or 66 percent) of them enabled only one signature network and its affiliated PIN network. Such banks likely added another PIN network to their cards to comply with Regulation II.

[155] In its rule proposal, the Federal Reserve considered requiring issuers to allow at least two unaffiliated signature networks and two unaffiliated PIN networks to process their debit card transactions. 75 Fed. Reg. 81,722 (Dec. 28, 2010). The Federal Reserve rejected this possibility in the final rule.

[156] According to their published interchange fee schedules as of October 29, 2012, both VISA and MasterCard have set debit interchange fees for covered transactions at the mandated cap.

[157] An issuer bank could choose to allow one signature and one unaffiliated PIN network on its cards and still be in compliance with Regulation II. In this case, Regulation II provides only one choice for routing once the customer decides to conduct a PIN or a signature transaction.

[158] As mentioned earlier, the recent antitrust settlement between the Department of Justice and VISA and MasterCard requires the card networks to allow merchants accepting cards by those networks to offer a discount to customers to completing their debit transactions using their PIN rather than signature.

[159] VISA representatives have explained publicly that this new fee structure is a strategic response to Regulation II. They said that VISA's PIN network, Interlink, lost significant transaction volume due to Regulation II, and the new fee structure is one of the company's strategies to regain some of the lost market share. VISA representatives stated that on March 13, 2012, the Department of Justice Antitrust Division issued a civil investigative demand requesting additional information about the company's debit strategies, including this fixed acquirer fee.

[160] According to experts, merchants likely will pay the new fixed fee since most will not want to refuse customer payments made with VISA cards.

[161] Representatives from VISA said this move was a strategic response to their loss of market share associated with Regulation II. VISA representatives stated that on March 13, 2012, the Department of Justice Antitrust Division issued a civil investigative demand requesting additional information about the company's debit strategies, including information about the VISA signature debit network's ability to authenticate PIN transactions.

[162] The interchange fee standard provides that a covered issuer bank may not receive or charge an interchange transaction fee in excess of the sum of a 21-cent base component and 5 basis points of the transaction's value. 76 Fed. Reg. 43,394.

In: The Dodd-Frank Act
Editor: Candace Edmonds

ISBN: 978-1-62618-050-5

Chapter 2

THE DODD-FRANK WALL STREET REFORM AND CONSUMER PROTECTION ACT: ISSUES AND SUMMARY*

Baird Webel

SUMMARY

Beginning in 2007, U.S. financial conditions deteriorated, leading to the near collapse of the U.S. financial system in September 2008. Major banks, insurers, government-sponsored enterprises, and investment banks either failed or required hundreds of billions in federal support to continue functioning.

Households were hit hard by drops in the prices of real estate and financial assets, and by a sharp rise in unemployment. Congress responded to the crisis by enacting the most comprehensive financial reform legislation since the 1930s.

Treasury Secretary Timothy Geithner issued a reform plan in the summer of 2009, which served as a template for legislation in both the House and Senate.

House committees reported a number of bills on an issue-by-issue basis, which were then consolidated into a comprehensive bill, the Wall Street Reform and Consumer Protection Act of 2009 (H.R. 4173). H.R. 4173, as passed by the House on December 11, 2009, contained elements

* This is an edited, reformatted and augmented version of a Congressional Research Services publication, R41350, dated July 29, 2010.

of H.R. 1728, H.R. 2571, H.R. 2609, H.R. 3126, H.R. 3269, H.R. 3817, H.R. 3818, H.R. 3890, and H.R. 3996. On May 20, 2010, the Senate passed H.R. 4173, after substituting the text of Senator Christopher Dodd's bill, the Restoring American Financial Stability Act of 2010 (S. 3217), as amended.

Following a conference committee, the House accepted changes to H.R. 4173, now titled the Dodd-Frank Wall Street Reform and Consumer Protection Act, on June 30, 2010, and the Senate followed suit on July 15, 2010. President Obama signed the bill, now P.L. 111-203, on July 21, 2010.

Perhaps the major issue in financial reform has been how to address the systemic fragility that was revealed by the crisis. The Dodd-Frank Act creates a new regulatory umbrella group chaired by the Treasury Secretary—the Financial Stability Oversight Council—with authority to designate certain financial firms as "systemically significant" and subjecting them to increased prudential regulation, including limits on leverage, heightened capital standards, and restrictions on certain forms of risky trading.

These firms will also be subject to a special resolution process similar to that used in the past to address failing depository institutions.

Other aspects of financial reform address particular sectors of the financial system or selected classes of market participants. The Dodd-Frank Act consolidates consumer protection responsibilities in a new Bureau of Consumer Financial Protection within the Federal Reserve. The act consolidates bank regulation by merging the Office of Thrift Supervision (OTS) into the Office of the Comptroller of the Currency (OCC).

It requires more derivatives to be cleared and traded through regulated exchanges, and it mandates reporting for derivatives that remain in the over-the-counter market. Hedge funds have new reporting and registration requirements.

Credit rating agencies are subject to greater disclosure and legal liability provisions, and references to credit ratings will be removed from statute and regulation. A federal office is created to collect insurance information. Executive compensation and securitization reforms attempt to reduce incentives to take excessive risks. Intermediaries who provide investment advice to retail investors and municipalities may be subject to a fiduciary duty.

The Federal Reserve's emergency authority is amended and its activities are subject to greater public disclosure and oversight by the Government Accountability Office (GAO).

This report reviews issues related to financial regulation and provides brief descriptions of major provisions of the Dodd-Frank Act.

INTRODUCTION

Comprehensive Financial Reform Proposals

The 111th Congress considered several proposals to reorganize financial regulators and to reform the regulation of financial markets and financial institutions. Following House committee markups on various bills addressing specific issues, House Committee on Financial Services Chairman Barney Frank introduced the Wall Street Reform and Consumer Protection Act of 2009 (H.R. 4173), incorporating elements of numerous previous bills.[1] After two days of floor consideration, the House passed H.R. 4173 on December 11, 2009, on a vote of 232-202.

Chairman Christopher Dodd of the Senate Committee on Banking, Housing, and Urban Affairs issued a single comprehensive committee print on November 16, 2009, the Restoring American Financial Stability Act of 2009.[2] This proposal was revised over the following months and a committee print of the Restoring American Financial Stability Act of 2010[3] was issued on March 15, 2010. This bill was amended in committee on March 22, 2010, and was reported as S. 3217 on April 15, 2010. The full Senate took up S. 3217 and amended it several times, finishing consideration on May 20, 2010, when it substituted the text of S. 3217 into H.R. 4173. The Senate then passed its version of H.R. 4173 on a vote of 59-39.

Following a conference committee, the House on June 30, 2010, agreed to the H.R. 4173conference report—now titled the Dodd-Frank Wall Street Reform and Consumer Protection Act—by a vote of 237-192. The Senate agreed to the report on July 15, 2010, by a vote of 60-39. The legislation was signed into law on July 21, 2010, as P.L. 111-203.

In addition to Chairman Dodd's and Chairman Frank's bills, other proposals were made but not scheduled for markup. For example, House Financial Services Committee Ranking Member Spencer Bachus introduced a comprehensive reform proposal, the Consumer Protection and Regulatory Enhancement Act (H.R. 3310), and offered a similar amendment (H.Amdt. 539) during House consideration of H.R. 4173.[4] In March 2008, Treasury Secretary Hank Paulson issued a "Blueprint for a Modernized Financial Regulatory Structure."[5] The Obama Administration released "Financial Regulatory Reform: A New Foundation" in June 2009, and followed this with specific legislative language that provided a base text for congressional consideration.[6]

This report discusses related major provisions of the enacted version of the Dodd-Frank Act.

Understanding the fabric of financial reform proposals requires some analysis both of the Panic of 2008, as well as of more enduring concerns about risks in the financial system. This report begins with that analysis.

The Panic of September 2008[7]

The financial disruptions that peaked in September 2008 focused policy attention on systemic risk, which had previously been a subject of interest to academics and central bankers, but was not seen as a significant threat to economic stability. The last major systemic risk episode was bank runs in the Great Depression; the main elements of the current bank regulatory regime and federal safety net were put in place to prevent its recurrence. Between the end of the Great Depression and the early 2000s, the financial system weathered numerous shocks, failures, and crashes, with limited spillover into the real economy. Typically, the Federal Reserve (Fed) would announce that it stood ready to provide liquidity to the system, and that proved sufficient to stem panic. The idea that a financial shock could cause the entire system to spin out of control and collapse, and that the flow of credit might stop altogether, seemed to many to be a remote prospect. De facto policy was to rely on the Fed to deal with crises after the fact.

The events of 2007 and 2008 caused a sharp reassessment of the robustness and the self-stabilizing capacity of the financial system. As Treasury Secretary Timothy Geithner noted in written testimony delivered to the House Financial Services Committee on September 23, 2009, "The job of the financial system ... is to efficiently allocate savings and risk. Last fall, our financial system failed to do its job, and came precariously close to failing altogether."[8]

A number of discrete failures in individual markets and institutions led to global financial panic. U.S. financial firms suffered heavy losses in 2007 and 2008, primarily because of declines in the value of mortgage-related assets. During September 2008, Fannie Mae and Freddie Mac were placed in government conservatorship. Merrill Lynch was sold in distress to Bank of America in a deal supported by the Fed and Treasury. The Fed and Treasury failed to find a buyer for Lehman Brothers, which subsequently filed for bankruptcy, disrupting financial markets. A money market mutual fund (the Reserve Primary Fund) that held Lehman-related paper announced losses, triggering a run on other money market funds, and Treasury responded with a guarantee for money market funds. The American International Group (AIG), an insurance conglomerate with a securities subsidiary that specialized in financial derivatives, including credit default swaps, was unable to post collateral related to its derivatives and securities lending activities. The Fed intervened with an $85 billion loan to prevent bankruptcy and to ensure full payment to AIG's counterparties. In response to the general panic, Congress approved the $700 billion Troubled Asset Relief Program (TARP); the Fed introduced several lending facilities to provide liquidity to different parts of the financial system; and the Federal Deposit Insurance Corporation (FDIC) introduced a debt guarantee program for banks. The panic largely subsided through the latter part of 2008, although confidence in the financial system returned very slowly.

It was widely understood that the panic had its roots in the subprime mortgage market, in which years of double-digit housing price increases had fed a bubble mentality and caused lenders to relax their customary prudence. That the housing market would cool, as it began to do in 2006, was not a great surprise. What was generally unexpected was the way losses caused by rising foreclosures and bad loan rippled through the system. Major financial institutions had constructed highly leveraged speculative positions that magnified the subprime shock, so that a setback in a $1 trillion segment of the U.S. housing market generated many times that amount in financial losses.

Giant financial institutions were shown to be vulnerable to liquidity runs, and many failed or had to be rescued as short-term credit dried up. The value of complex financial instruments created through securitization became completely uncertain, and market participants lost confidence in each others' creditworthiness. Risks that were thought to be unrelated became highly correlated; a negative spiral that showed all financial risk taking to be interconnected and all declines to be self-reinforcing took hold. Doubts about counterparty exposure were magnified by opacity in derivatives markets.

Disruption to the financial system exacerbated recessionary forces already at work in the economy. Asset prices plunged and consumers suffered sharp losses in their retirement and college savings accounts, as well as in the value of their homes. The financial crisis accelerated declines in consumption and business investment, which in turn made banks' problems worse. Overall, the recession proved to be the deepest and longest since the Great Depression.

Against this background, Congress took up financial reform legislation in 2009. The legislation included measures to improve systemic stability, improve policy options for coping with failing financial firms, increase transparency throughout financial markets, and protect consumers and investors. By the time of final passage, the Dodd-Frank Act included provisions that affect virtually every financial market and to amend existing or grant new authority and responsibility to nearly every federal financial regulatory agency.

THE DODD-FRANK ACT (P.L. 111-203)

Systemic Risk

Policy Issues[9]

Systemic risk refers to sources of instability for the financial system as a whole, often through "contagion" or "spillover" effects that individual firms cannot protect themselves against.[10] Although regulators took systemic risk into account before the crisis, and systemic risk can never be eliminated, analysts have pointed to a number of ostensible weaknesses in the regulatory regime's approach to systemic risk. First, there has been no regulator with overarching responsibility for mitigating systemic risk. Some analysts argue that systemic risk can fester in the gaps in the regulatory system where one regulator's jurisdiction ends and another's begins. Second, the crisis revealed that liquidity crises and runs were not just a problem for depository institutions. Third, the crisis revealed that nonbank, highly leveraged firms, such as Lehman Brothers and AIG, could be a source of systemic risk and "too big (or too interconnected) to fail." Finally, there were concerns that the breakdown of different payment, clearing, and settlement (PCS) systems, which are not regulated consistently (or, in some cases, at all), would be another source of systemic risk.

Provisions in the Dodd-Frank Act (Titles I and VIII)

The Dodd-Frank Act does not create a dedicated systemic risk regulator with powers to neutralize sources of systemic risk as they arise. Instead, it creates a Financial Services Oversight Council (FSOC), chaired by the Treasury Secretary and consisting of eight heads of federal regulatory agencies (including the newly created Consumer Financial Protection Bureau) and a presidential appointee with insurance experience. The act creates an Office of Financial Research to support the council. The council is authorized to identify and advise regulators on sources of systemic risk and "regulatory gap" problems, but would have no rulemaking, examination, or enforcement powers of its own. The council is to identify systemically important financial firms regardless of their legal charter, and the Fed will subject them to stricter prudential oversight and regulation, including short-term debt limits, a 10% liability concentration limit, counterparty exposure set at 25% of total capital, risk-based capital requirements (that account for off-balance sheet activities), annual stress tests, and a 15-to-1 leverage limit. The details of this stricter oversight will be determined by the Fed in yet-to-be issued implementing rules. Many large firms are already regulated by the Fed for safety and soundness because they are bank holding companies; the act prevents a firm from changing its charter in order to escape Fed regulation. In addition, the Dodd-Frank Act includes mechanisms by which the Fed would be empowered to curb the growth or reduce the size of large firms to prevent systemic risk.

The Dodd-Frank Act (Section 619) puts limits on commercial banks' proprietary trading activities and investments in hedge funds or private equity firms.[11] It also provides for many PCS systems and activities deemed systemically important by the council to be regulated by the Fed, unless those systems are registered with the Securities and Exchange Commission (SEC) or the Commodities Futures Trading Commission (CFTC), in which case the system would be regulated by those entities. Title XI would also allow the FDIC to set up emergency liquidity programs to guarantee the debt of bank holding companies, similar to the 2008 Temporary Liquidity Guarantee Program.

Federal Reserve Emergency Authority and Congressional Oversight

Policy Issues[12]

During the recent financial turmoil, the Fed engaged in unprecedented levels of emergency lending to nonbank financial firms through its authority under Section 13(3) of the Federal Reserve Act. This statute states that "in unusual and exigent circumstances, the Board of Governors of the Federal Reserve System, by the affirmative vote of not less than five members, may authorize any Federal reserve bank ... to discount for any individual, partnership, or corporation, notes, drafts, and bills of exchange...."[13]

Such loans can be made only if secured to the Fed's satisfaction and if the targeted borrower is unable to obtain the needed credit through other banking institutions. In addition to the level of lending, the form of the lending has been novel, particularly the creation of three limited liability corporations controlled by the Fed, to which the Fed lent a total of $72.6 billion to purchase illiquid assets from Bear Stearns and AIG. The Fed's recent actions under Section 13(3) generated debate in Congress about whether measures were needed to amend the institution's emergency lending powers.

Provisions in the Dodd-Frank Act (Title XI)

The Dodd-Frank Act includes several provisions related to Federal Reserve lending authority. In particular, this legislation stipulates that, although the Fed may authorize a Federal Reserve Bank to make collateralized loans as part of a broadly available credit facility, it may not authorize a Federal Reserve Bank to lend to only a single and specific individual, partnership, or corporation. When using emergency authority, the Fed will be required to seek approval from the Treasury Secretary. In addition, the Dodd-Frank Act allows the Government Accountability Office (GAO) to audit the Fed's lending facilities and open market operations for internal controls and risk management, and it calls for a GAO audit of the Fed's actions during the crisis. The act requires disclosure of Fed borrowers and borrowing terms, with a lag. The act also prohibits firms regulated by the Fed from participating in the selection of directors of the regional Federal Reserve Banks.

Resolution Regime for Failing Firms

Policy Issues[14]

Most companies that fail in the United States are resolved in accordance with the bankruptcy code. Depository institutions that hold FDIC-insured deposits are subject to a special resolution regime, called a conservatorship or receivership. Under normal circumstances, bankruptcies are judicial in nature with no additional public resources available to support the process. The FDIC's conservatorship/receivership regime is a largely nonjudicial, administrative process, requiring the FDIC to resolve depositories such that the total to be expended will cost the Deposit Insurance Fund less than any other possible method. Under limited circumstances, the FDIC may waive this "least-cost resolution" requirement in order to minimize systemic risk.[15] Some believe that the speed and discretion available in the FDIC's conservatorship/receivership regime is a useful model for resolving other types of systemically important financial firms. The collapse of Lehman Brothers (and the near collapse of AIG, Bear Stearns, and others) during the recent financial crisis has focused congressional attention on policy options for resolving systemically significant nondepository financial institutions.[16] Proponents argue that creating a special resolution regime for such firms would make future taxpayer bailouts unnecessary. Opponents argue that it would provide a way for policymakers to provide "backdoor bailouts" to favored creditors and counterparties of failing firms.

Provisions in the Dodd-Frank Act (Title II)

The Dodd-Frank Act establishes a new system for certain financial companies whose resolution under otherwise available law is determined by various federal regulators to pose dangers to the U.S. financial system. This resolution system is modeled after the FDIC's existing receivership regime for depository institutions. Many types of financial companies and their subsidiaries are eligible for this special resolution regime; however, subsidiaries that are insurance companies, certain broker-dealers, and insured depositories are not eligible.

For an eligible financial company to be resolved under the special regime, a group of regulators, including two-thirds of the Federal Reserve Board, must recommend the company for the resolution based on standards delineated by the Dodd-Frank Act. After the recommendation, the Secretary of the Treasury (Secretary), in consultation with the President, must make a determination that the "company is in default or in danger of default;" the company's resolution under otherwise available law would "have serious adverse effects on financial stability of the United States; no viable private sector alternative is available;" and other considerations.[17] A company that disputes the determination by the Secretary will have limited rights to appeal the determination in federal court.

Although the special resolution regime is modeled after the FDIC's receivership power, there are some important distinctions between the two. For instance, the Dodd-Frank Act emphasizes that

> creditors and shareholders will bear the losses of the financial company; management responsible for the condition of the financial company will not be retained; and the [FDIC] and other appropriate regulators will take all steps necessary and appropriate to assure that all parties ... having responsibility for the condition of the financial company bear losses consistent with their responsibility, including actions for damages, restitution, and recoupment of compensation and other gains not compatible with such responsibility.[18]

The act also states that "[a]ll financial companies put into receivership under this title shall be liquidated, [and n]o taxpayer funds shall be used to prevent the liquidation of any financial company under this title."[19]

The funding mechanism for resolutions under the Dodd-Frank Act also differs from the conservatorship/receivership regime for depositories. The Orderly Liquidation Fund established by the Dodd-Frank Act will not be prefunded. Instead, the FDIC, upon being appointed receiver of a particular financial company, is authorized to borrow funds from the Treasury subject to explicit caps based on the value of the failed firm's consolidated assets. If necessary to pay off such obligations to the Treasury, the FDIC would have the authority to assess claimants of the failed institution that received more compensation through the receivership than they would have received had the failed firm been liquidated in bankruptcy, as well as with the power to assess certain large financial institutions (bank holding companies and nonbank financial companies eligible for the special resolution regime that have more than $50 billion in assets and all nonbank financial institutions supervised by the Fed as systemically significant). The Dodd-Frank Act also imposes a three-year time limit on any receivership with the possibility of up to two one-year extensions.

Securitization and Shadow Banking

Policy Issues[20]

Shadow banking refers to financial activity either conducted by nonbanks or sponsored by banks off of their balance sheets. Securitization supports the shadow banking system. Securitization is the process of turning mortgages, credit card loans, and other debt into marketable securities. Securitizers acquire and pool many loans from primary lenders and then issue new securities based on the flow of payments through the pool. This process can allow banks to reduce the risk of their retained portfolios. Securitization also finances nonbank lenders specializing in mortgage loans, credit cards, and other loan products, and thus can increase the amount of credit available to businesses and consumers. If the risks of securitized products are adequately managed and understood, securitization can enhance financial stability by shifting financial risk to those most willing and able to bear it.

Securitization risks were not properly managed during the period leading up to the crisis, which contributed to the housing bubble and financial turmoil in a variety of ways. Lenders planning to sell their loans have a reduced stake in the borrower's long-term capacity to repay the loan. Bank underwriting standards are subject to guidances issued by bank regulators because loans to risky borrowers might be unsafe and unsound for the banks themselves. These guidances, however, do not apply to nonbank mortgage lenders that are funded through securitization (although the Fed has separate authority to regulate lending).

Private securitization was especially prevalent in the subprime mortgage market, the nonconforming mortgage market, and in regions where loan defaults have been particularly severe. As loans were made that the lender never expected to hold, mortgage underwriting standards deteriorated.

Opaqueness in the shadow banking system also caused problems. When defaults rose among home buyers, the complexity of mortgage-backed securities (MBSs) made it more difficult to identify which firms would suffer the largest losses.

Furthermore, a drop in the credit rating of a MBS could require some holders to sell, even though the security was still performing. In addition to holding the securities of nonbank subprime lenders, some banks also sponsored their own mortgage funding facilities off their balance sheets in special purpose vehicles. When the liquidity of MBSs declined, some of these sponsoring banks had to pull the assets of such special purpose vehicles back on to their balance sheets and recognize more losses.

One approach to address incentives in securitization is to require loan securitizers to retain a portion of the long-term default risk. An advantage of this "skin in the game" requirement is that it may help preserve underwriting standards among lenders funded by securitization. Another advantage is that securitizers would share in the risks faced by the investors to whom they market their securities.

A possible disadvantage is that if each step of the securitization chain must retain a portion of risk, then relatively little risk may ultimately be shifted out of the financial sector to investors. To the extent that securitization is seen as a device to shift risk to those more willing and able to bear it, concentration of risk in the financial sector may be self-defeating.

Provisions in the Dodd-Frank Act (Title IX)

The Dodd-Frank Act generally requires securitizers to retain some of the risk if they issue asset-backed securities. The amount of risk required to be retained depends in part on the quality of the underlying assets. Regulators are instructed to write risk retention rules requiring less than 5% retained risk if the securitized assets meet prescribed underwriting standards. For assets that do not meet these standards, regulators are instructed to require not less than 5% retention of risk. Securitizers are prohibited from hedging the retained credit risk.

The Dodd-Frank Act requires separate risk retention rules for different asset classes that are securitized (residential mortgages, commercial mortgages, auto loans, etc.).

The risk retention rules for securitization of nonmortgage assets are to be jointly issued by the SEC and Federal Banking Agencies (FDIC, Office of the Comptroller of the Currency [OCC], and Federal Reserve). The risk retention rules for the securitization of mortgage assets are to be jointly issued by the SEC, the Federal Banking Agencies, the Department of Housing and Urban Development (HUD), and the Federal Housing Finance Agency (FHFA). Regulators are also directed to craft risk retention rules appropriate to collateralized debt obligations (CDOs) and other complex securities if the underlying assets are tranches of other asset-backed securities.

Regulators may also impose retained risk requirements on originators of assets after taking into account the riskiness of the assets, whether securitization markets are causing a decline in prudent underwriting, and the effect on the ability of consumers and businesses to obtain credit on reasonable terms.

In the case of residential mortgages that are securitized, the Dodd-Frank Act allows for a complete exemption from risk retention if all of the mortgages in the securitization meet the standards of a "qualified residential mortgage," which regulators will define according to certain factors, but which must be no broader than the definition of "qualified mortgage" in Section 1412 of Dodd-Frank.

Some of the factors are full documentation of borrowers' financial resources, debt-to-income ratio limits, and payment shock mitigation. The act also provides an exemption from retained risk requirements for certain Farm Credit Administration loans and related guarantees. Also exempt are loans guaranteed by the United States or an agency of the United States, as well as municipal securities. Notably, securities guaranteed by Fannie Mae and Freddie Mac are not automatically exempt.

The act requires securitizers to perform due diligence on the underlying assets of the securitization and to disclose the nature of the due diligence. In addition, investors in asset-backed securities are to receive more information about the underlying assets.

Consolidation of Bank Supervision

Policy Issues[21]

Commercial banks and similar institutions are subject to regulatory examination for safety and soundness. Prior to the crisis, depending on their charter, commercial banks, thrifts, and credit unions may have been examined by the OCC, the Office of Thrift Supervision (OTS), the Federal Reserve, the National Credit Union Administration (NCUA), or a state authority. State bank examiners often coordinated through the Conference of State Bank Supervisors. Federal bank examiners often conducted joint rulemaking and coordinated through the Federal Financial Institutions Examinations Council (FFIEC). In addition, some firms engage in bank-like activities, but are not subject to oversight by bank regulators.

The system of multiple bank regulators was believed to have problems, some of which could be mitigated by regulatory consolidation. Multiple regulators may find it challenging to implement consistent enforcement even if they employ joint rulemaking. To the extent that regulations are applied inconsistently, institutions may have an incentive to choose the regulator that they feel will be the weakest or least intrusive. If so, competition among the regulators for covered institutions (regulatory arbitrage) could lead to less effective financial supervision. Among the arguments against consolidation are that regulatory consolidation could change the traditional U.S. dual banking system in ways that put smaller banks at a disadvantage. Another argument for maintaining the current system is that competition among regulators encourages the regulators to monitor each other and alert policymakers if one regulator lowers standards.

During the Dodd-Frank policy debate, there was concern about the Fed's roles in both bank holding company regulation and conducting monetary policy. Some argued that the Fed should concentrate on monetary policy and have fewer regulatory responsibilities, especially if the institution's independence is to be preserved. In contrast, the Fed argued that its bank regulation responsibilities provided it with helpful information for the conduct of monetary policy.

Provisions in the Dodd-Frank Act (Title III)

The Dodd-Frank Act did not effect a complete consolidation of banking agencies, nor did it remove the Fed's bank regulatory responsibilities. Title III eliminates the Office of Thrift Supervision as an independent agency and reassigns its duties to the FDIC, the OCC, and to the Federal Reserve. The Fed will be the holding company level regulator for institutions formerly regulated by OTS. The OCC will be the depository institution level regulator for federally chartered thrifts. The FDIC will be the depository institution level regulator for state chartered thrifts. The Fed remains the regulator for state chartered member banks. Title III also expands the assessment base for the FDIC's deposit insurance fund. The new formula will be based upon the total assets of the insured depository minus the average tangible equity of the insured depository. Title VI also creates a three-year moratorium on chartering new credit card banks, industrial loan companies, and trust banks.

Consumer Financial Protection[22]

Policy Issues

In the United States, depository institutions—banks, thrifts, and credit unions—have been subject to comprehensive supervision, examination, and enforcement by a number of federal regulators. These regulators have monitored the institutions that they supervise for both safety and soundness and for compliance with other federal laws, including the various federal consumer protection laws. Many nondepository financial companies, such as payday lenders and nonbank mortgage lenders, have been primarily regulated by the states. However, the financial products that these nondepositories offer may still be subject to federal consumer protection laws, such as the Truth in Lending Act (TILA).[23] The Federal Reserve largely has been charged with promulgating the regulations to implement the TILA and most other federal consumer protection laws, and the Federal Trade Commission (FTC) primarily has been responsible for enforcing these laws and regulations against institutions that do not have a primary federal regulator.

In light of this fragmented system, some have proposed legislation to consolidate consumer financial protection functions. These proposals raise policy questions regarding how best to balance safety and soundness regulation with consumer compliance. Although a loan that cannot be repaid is typically bad for both the borrower and the lender, there are some areas in which there can be a conflict between safety and soundness regulation and consumer protection. When a banking activity is profitable, safety and soundness regulators tend to look upon it favorably, because it enables the bank to meet capital requirements and withstand financial shocks. A consumer protection regulator, however, may look at such activity less favorably, especially if the profit is seen to have been gained unfairly at the expense of consumers. Removing consumer compliance authority from the federal bank regulators may weaken the safety and soundness regulation of banks if, for example, the separation results in a less complete picture of bank operations for the prudential regulator. The Fed has argued that its role in consumer protection aids its other authorities, including bank supervision and systemic risk. On the other hand, some, including the Obama Administration, have argued that professional bank examiners are trained "to see the world through the lenses of institutions and markets, not consumers,"[24] and separating compliance and safety and soundness into a different agency is the best way to protect both consumers and financial institutions. The extent to which the cost and availability of credit will be affected by a new regulator will depend on exactly what rules it prescribes and how aggressively it and the other regulators enforce consumer protection laws and regulations.

Provisions in the Dodd-Frank Act (Title X)

The Dodd-Frank Act establishes a Bureau of Consumer Financial Protection within the Federal Reserve System to have authority over an array of consumer financial products and services (including deposit taking, mortgages, credit cards and other extensions of credit, loan servicing, check-guaranteeing, collection of consumer report data, debt collection, real estate settlement, money transmitting, financial data processing, among others). It will serve as the primary federal consumer financial protection supervisor and enforcer of federal consumer protection laws over many of the institutions that offer these products and services. The bureau will be required to consult with the prudential regulators when prescribing regulations.

The bureau's authority over financial institutions varies according to the type of company: (1) depository institutions with more than $10 billion in assets (i.e., "larger depositories"); (2) depositories institutions with $10 billion or less in assets (i.e., "smaller depositories"); and (3) nondepositories. The Dodd-Frank Act explicitly exempts a number of different entities and consumer financial activities from the bureau's supervisory and enforcement authority. Within a year and a half of enactment, primary consumer protection supervisory and enforcement powers over larger depositories that are currently held in those institutions' prudential regulators will be transferred to the bureau.

The bureau will not acquire primary supervisory and enforcement powers over smaller depositories. Instead, these powers will remain with those institutions' primary regulators. The bureau will have some ability to participate in the examination of these smaller depositories, refer potential enforcement actions against smaller depository institutions to their prudential regulators, and require reports directly from these depositories. While the bureau's supervisory and enforcement powers are limited with regard to these smaller depositories, they, along with their larger depository counterparts, generally will be subject to the consumer protection rules prescribed by the bureau.

Regarding nondepository institutions that offer consumer financial products and services, the bureau would only be the primary supervisor and enforcer over entities that

1) are engaged in consumer mortgage related activities (i.e., mortgage origination, brokerage, or servicing activities, mortgage modification or foreclosure relief activities);
2) are nonmortgage related consumer financial entities that are "larger participant[s] in a market" as determined by the Bureau in regulations and after consultation with the FTC;
3) the Bureau has reasonable cause to believe are "engaging, or ha[ve] engaged, in conduct that poses risks to consumers with regard to the offering or provision of consumer financial products or services;"
4) provide or offer to provide private student loans; or
5) provide or offer to provide a payday loan.[25]

The bureau's supervisory powers over these covered nondepositories include the authority to require them to register with the bureau, submit to background checks, or adhere to other measures "to ensure that such persons are legitimate entities and are able to perform their obligations to consumers."[26]

The Dodd-Frank Act authorizes the bureau to prescribe rules and issue orders and guidance. The act also transfers to the bureau rulemaking authority for many of the existing federal consumer protection laws (referred to as the "enumerated consumer laws"), including the TILA, Real Estate Settlement Procedures Act, and Home Ownership and Equity Protection Act. As a check on the bureau's rulemaking powers, the Financial Stability Oversight Council has the ability to set aside a regulation prescribed by the bureau if the regulation "would put the safety and soundness of the United States banking system or the stability of the financial system of the United States at risk."

As previously mentioned, the Dodd-Frank Act explicitly exempts some activities and entities from the bureau's jurisdiction. For instance, the bureau generally will not have any power to regulate insurance activities or to impose interest rate caps on products. The act also significantly limits the bureau's supervisory, enforcement, and rulemaking powers over a

> merchant, retailer, or seller of nonfinancial goods or services ... to the extent that such person (i) extends credit directly to a consumer ... exclusively for the purpose of enabling that consumer to purchase such nonfinancial good or service directly from the merchant, retailer, or seller; (ii) ... collects debt arising from [such] credit ... or (iii) sells or conveys [such] debt ... that is delinquent or otherwise in default.[27]

The bureau's authority is further restricted on certain merchants, retailers, and sellers of nonfinancial goods that are also small businesses. It generally does not have supervisory, rulemaking, or enforcement powers over automobile dealers, but the Dodd-Frank Act makes it easier for the FTC to regulate them.[28] Other entities for which the act provides certain exemptions include real estate brokers, real estate agents, sellers of manufactured and mobile homes, income tax preparers, and accountants, each to the extent that they are acting in their normal capacity (e.g., a real estate broker would be exempt to the extent that s/he brings parties together to purchase a property). However, the bureau will be able to exert authority over these entities to the extent that they are subject to an enumerated consumer law.

Mortgage Standards

Policy Issues

Beginning around the middle of 2006, residential mortgage delinquency and foreclosure rates began to rise sharply in many regions of the United States. In addition to the negative effects on some homeowners, the increase in nonperforming mortgages contributed to the financial crisis by straining the balance sheets of financial firms that held those mortgages. Although all kinds of mortgages experienced increases in delinquency and foreclosure, many poorly performing mortgages exhibited increasingly complex features, such as adjustable interest rates, or nontraditional mortgage features, such as negative amortization.[29] Such nontraditional or complex mortgage features may be appropriate for some borrowers in some circumstances, many were made available more widely than the purposes for which they were originally intended. In addition, some observers view certain mortgage features, such as high prepayment penalties, as predatory. Although not all troubled mortgages exhibited these or similar features, and not all loans that exhibited such features became troubled, some observers point to the widespread use of such mortgage terms as having exacerbated the housing "bubble" and its subsequent collapse.

The role that nonperforming mortgages played in the recent financial crisis have led some to suggest that actions should be taken both to protect consumers from risky mortgage products and to protect the U.S. financial system from experiencing major losses due to troubled mortgages in the future. One possible way to minimize mortgage defaults and foreclosures is to limit or prohibit certain mortgage features that are viewed as especially risky. Another would be to require mortgage lenders to offer consumers basic mortgage products with traditional terms alongside any loan with nontraditional features. Although either of these approaches may reduce the chances of widespread mortgage failures, and might help preserve financial stability, both could also limit consumer choice or prevent borrowers from taking out loans with nontraditional features that may be advantageous given their specific circumstances. Some argue that such approaches could limit financial innovation in mortgage products or reduce competition among lenders.

Provisions in the Dodd-Frank Act (Title XIV)

The Dodd-Frank Act amends the Truth in Lending Act to set minimum standards for certain residential mortgages. Lenders will be required to determine that mortgage borrowers have a reasonable ability to repay the mortgages that they receive, based on the borrowers' verified income and other factors, subject to regulations promulgated by the Fed. Certain "qualified mortgages" with traditional mortgage terms will be presumed to have met these requirements. The Fed is also directed to issue regulations prohibiting mortgage originators from "steering" consumers to mortgages that (1) those consumers do not have a reasonable ability to repay, (2) exhibit certain features that are determined to be predatory, or (3) meet certain other conditions. It is also directed to issue regulations prohibiting any practices related to residential mortgage lending that it deems to be "abusive, unfair, deceptive, [or] predatory." The legislation restricts the use of prepayment penalties. Mortgage originators are prohibited from receiving compensation that varies in any way based on the applicable mortgages terms or conditions, other than the principal amount. The legislation also requires increased disclosures to consumers on a range of topics, including disclosures related to how certain features of a mortgage may affect the consumer.

New requirements related to "high-cost mortgages" are included in the legislation, such as limitations on the terms of such mortgages and a requirement that lenders verify that borrowers have received pre-purchase counseling before obtaining such a mortgage. The legislation also imposes additional restrictions on residential mortgage loans and includes additional housing-related provisions that are not discussed in this report.

Derivatives

Policy Issues[30]

Derivatives are financial contracts whose value is linked to some underlying price or variable. Derivatives are traded both on organized exchanges with central clearing houses that guarantee payment on all contracts, and in a previously unregulated over-the-counter (OTC) market, where credit risk is borne by the individual counterparties. The CFTC regulates commodity futures and options on futures, whereas the SEC regulates options on securities.

The Commodity Futures Modernization Act of 2000 (CFMA) [31] largely exempted swaps and other derivatives in the OTC market from regulation. The collapse of AIG in 2008 illustrated the risks of large OTC derivatives positions that are not backed by collateral or margin (as a central clearing house would require). If AIG had been required to post margin on its credit default swap contracts, it would not have been able to build such a large position, which may have reduced the threat to systemic stability and resulting a costly taxpayer bailout. Such disruptions in markets for financial derivatives during the recent crisis led to calls for changes in derivatives regulation, particularly in the OTC market. Further, opacity in the OTC market made it difficult for policymakers and market participants to gauge firms' risk exposures, arguably exacerbating the panic.

Derivatives reform focused on requiring the OTC markets to adopt features of the regulated markets, including mandatory clearing through derivatives clearing organizations, trading on exchanges or exchange-like facilities, registration of certain market participants, and the like.

Provisions in the Dodd-Frank Act (Titles VII and XVI)

The Dodd-Frank Act mandates centralized clearing and exchange-trading of many OTC derivatives, but provides exemptions for certain market participants.[32] The act creates a process by which federal regulators (either the

CFTC or the SEC) will determine which types of swaps and security-based swaps will be subject to the clearing requirement. It also requires reporting of all swaps and security-based swaps, including those that are not subject to or are exempt from the clearing requirement, to regulated entities or to regulators themselves. The act requires regulators to impose capital requirements on swap dealers, security-based swap dealers, major swap participants, and major security-based swaps participants. The CFTC is to regulate "swaps," which include contracts based on interest rates, currencies, physical commodities, some credit default swaps, whereas the SEC will have authority over "security-based swaps," including other credit default swaps and equity swaps.[33] Both agencies will be given the power to promulgate rules to prevent the evasion of the clearing requirements created by the act.

In general, swaps and security-based swaps that must be cleared must also be traded on an exchange or exchange-like facility that provides price transparency. The regulators are given considerable discretion to define the forms of trading that will meet this requirement.

The Dodd-Frank Act includes an exemption from the clearing requirement, if desired, if at least one party to the trade is an "end user,"[34] defined as parties that are not financial entities[35] and are using the swaps to hedge or mitigate commercial risk. An exempted party must inform the CFTC or SEC (depending on the contract) on how they generally meet their financial obligations when entering into noncleared swaps or security-based swaps.

Section 716, a widely debated section of the act, prohibits federal assistance to any swaps entity with respect to any swap, security-based swap, or other activity of the swaps entity.[36] Swaps entities are defined as swap dealers, security-based swap dealers, major swap participants, and major security-based swap participants that are registered under either the CEA or the Exchange Act. However, swap entities do not include any major swap participant or major security-based swap participant that is an insured depository institution. This exemption appears to address concerns that under previous language large commercial banks would have been unable to hedge their risk without becoming ineligible for federal assistance, including access to the Federal Reserve's discount window or any other Fed credit facility and FDIC insurance.

Depository institutions will be able to act as swap dealers in limited circumstances, such as when they are permitted to deal in the underlying interest, but not with regard to credit default swaps. Furthermore, depository institutions are permitted to establish an affiliate that is a swap entity as long as it is supervised by the Fed and comports with Sections 23A and 23B of the Federal Reserve Act.

Credit Rating Agencies

Policy Issues[37]

Credit rating agencies provide investors with an evaluation of the creditworthiness of bonds issued by a wide spectrum of entities, including corporations, sovereign nations, and municipalities. The grading of the creditworthiness is typically displayed in a letter hierarchical format: for example, AAA being the safest, with lower grades representing a greater risk. Credit rating agencies are typically paid by the issuers of the securities being rated by the agencies, which could be seen as a conflict of interest. In exchange for adhering to various reporting requirements, the SEC provides interested credit rating agencies with a Nationally Recognized Statistical Rating Organization (NRSRO) designation. The designation is particularly important because a variety of state and federal laws and regulations have referenced NRSRO ratings.[38]

In recent years, credit rating agencies have come under increased public scrutiny following several alleged performance failures. For instance, during the recent housing boom cycle the three dominant agencies (Fitch, Moody's, and Standard & Poor's) initially rated many mortgage-backed securities as AAA, before sharply downgrading the securities as the subprime mortgage market collapsed, resulting in heavy losses for investors that relied on these ratings. In some circumstances, downgrades forced financial firms to sell or hold more capital against the security, thereby exacerbating liquidity and deleveraging problems. The perceived agency failings have led to a focus on strengthening the accountability of credit rating agencies and reducing potential conflicts of interest that may compromise the integrity of their ratings.

Provisions in the Dodd-Frank Act (Title IX)

The Dodd-Frank Act contains provisions that enhance SEC regulation; impose new reporting, disclosure, and examination requirements on NRSROs; establish new standards of legal liability, create a new mechanism to prevent issuers of structured finance securities from choosing the agency that will perform the initial rating; and require removal of references to NRSRO ratings from federal statutes and regulations.

The act establishes an Office of Credit Ratings in the SEC to examine NRSROs and issue related regulations, including rules requiring that each credit rating be accompanied by extensive disclosures about the assumptions and methodologies underlying the rating. To permit users of ratings to compare NRSRO performance, the SEC will publish information on initial credit ratings and on subsequent changes to such ratings. After notice and opportunity for a hearing, the SEC will be permitted to temporarily suspend or permanently revoke an NRSRO's registration for a particular class of securities if it determines that the NRSRO lacks adequate financial and managerial resources for producing ratings with integrity.

Under the Dodd-Frank Act, NRSROs will be subject to the same standards of accountability as are statements made by registered public accounting firms and securities analysts. The act also permits investors to bring private rights of action against NRSROs for a knowing or reckless failure to conduct a reasonable investigation while performing a credit rating. The act requires the SEC to promulgate rules designed to prevent the sales and marketing considerations of an NRSRO from influencing the ratings that it produces and gives it the authority to revoke or suspend the registration of NRSROs that violated such rules.

The Dodd-Frank Act removes the references to credit ratings in selected sections in specific federal financial statutes.[39] Federal regulatory agencies will also be required to review and remove references to NRSRO ratings. The act also directs the SEC to conduct a study that would result in it establishing a system under which the initial rating assignments for structured finance securities would be made on a random or semirandom basis.

Investor Protection

Policy Issues

The multi-billion dollar Madoff Ponzi scheme raised concerns over the effectiveness of the SEC's efforts to protect investors. Madoff's operation was a registered broker-dealer subject to both SEC and Financial Industry Regulatory Authority (FINRA, the self regulatory organization for broker-dealers) oversight, as well as a registered investment adviser subject to SEC oversight. Reform initiatives seek to improve the SEC's performance by providing it with more funding and by amending the regulation of investment advisers and others.

Under prior law, broker-dealers were required to make recommendations "suitable" to their customers, while investment advisers have a fiduciary duty to act in the customers' best interests, without regard to their own compensation, and with an affirmative duty to disclose any potential conflicts of interest. The services provided by broker-dealers and investment advisers, however, often overlap—both can provide investment advice and there are some concerns that customers may falsely assume that the person advising them is committed to acting in their best interests.

Provisions in the Dodd-Frank Act (Title IX)

The Dodd-Frank Act gives the SEC the authority to impose a fiduciary duty on broker-dealers who offer personalized investment advice about securities to a retail customer following a study.

The SEC collects fees from securities transactions and registration fees, which go to an account available to congressional appropriators. The SEC's budget has often been much less than the annual fees that it collects and there has been interest in permitting the agency to be self-funded as is the case with the federal banking regulators. Under the Dodd-Frank Act, some fees will be available to appropriators to fund the SEC, while others will go to the Treasury General Fund. The SEC's budget will remain subject to the congressional appropriations process, but it will submit its budget request directly to Congress, without changes by the Administration. In addition, the Dodd-Frank Act authorizes increased funding levels for FY2011 to FY2015, subject to appropriations, which would result in almost a doubling of SEC funding. It also enables the SEC to access up to $100 million annually from a "Reserve Fund" for what the SEC "determines is necessary to carry out the functions of the agency,"[40] funded from the agency's fee collections.

The act creates an Office of Investor Advocate within the SEC. The Investor Advocate will assist retail investors in resolving significant problems they may have with the commission or with self-regulatory organizations; identify areas in which investors would benefit from changes in regulations; and identify problems that investors have with financial service providers and investment products.

The Dodd-Frank Act also establishes an Investor Advisory Committee within the SEC, whose purpose is to advise and consult with the SEC on regulatory priorities; issues relating to the regulation of securities products, trading strategies, fee structures, and the effectiveness of disclosure; initiatives to protect investor interest; and initiatives to promote investor confidence and the integrity of the securities marketplace. The committee will include an

Investor Advocate, a representative of the state securities commissions, senior citizen advocates, and persons representing the interests of individual equity and debt investors, and of institutional investors.

Previously, publicly traded corporations with a market value of less than $75 million (known as nonaccelerated filers) enjoyed a temporary exemption from Section 404(b) of the Sarbanes-Oxley Act of 2002, which requires publicly traded companies to audit their internal accounting controls (a process aimed at ensuring the reliability of a firm's financial reporting).[41] In 2009, the SEC adopted rules to remove the small company exemption, for the fiscal year ending on or after June 15, 2010. The Dodd-Frank Act effectively reverses that SEC rulemaking, making the exemption permanent.

The Dodd-Frank Act creates a new class of SEC registrant, the "municipal advisor." Intermediaries who provide financial advice to municipalities will be required to register with the SEC, abide by rules written by the Municipal Securities Rulemaking Board (MSRB), and will have a fiduciary duty to their clients. The MSRB membership will be reconstituted, so that board members who are independent of the municipal securities industry constitute a majority.

Hedge Funds

Policy Issues[42]

Hedge funds are not explicitly defined in federal securities law. They are generally described as privately organized, pooled investment vehicles not available to the public whose primary investors are wealthy individuals or institutions. Some hedge funds can also be distinguished from other investment funds by their pronounced use of leverage and their use of trading strategies based on short selling. The funds have a significant capital market presence. According to some estimates, they have been responsible for about one-fifth of the daily trading on the New York Stock Exchange and have over a trillion dollars in assets.

Hedge funds can provide benefits to financial markets by enhancing liquidity and efficiency and by reallocating financial risk. Some potential risks were revealed in 1998 when the hedge fund Long-Term Capital Management (LTCM) teetered on the brink of collapse. Concerns over the systemic implications of LTCM's collapse resulted in the New York Fed engineering a multibillion dollar rescue of the fund. Hedge fund failures did not play a prominent role in precipitating or spreading the recent financial crisis, however.

Under the "private adviser" exemption, hedge fund managers, who do not hold themselves to be investment advisers and who have fewer than 15 clients, have been exempted from registering with the SEC as investment advisers under the Investment Advisers Act (IAA).[43] Although some hedge fund managers registered voluntarily, it has been argued that the absence of comprehensive hedge fund data that would accompany mandatory fund registration, could deprive regulators of potentially critical information on the size and nature of the funds and the risks that they may or may not pose to the economy.

Provisions in the Dodd-Frank Act (Title IV)

The Dodd-Frank Act eliminates the "private adviser" exemption in the IAA, generally requiring advisers to private funds such as hedge funds with more than $150 million in assets under management to register with the SEC and to provide such information about their investment portfolios and strategies as the SEC and the FSOC deem necessary to monitor systemic risk. Advisers to venture capital funds and family offices (but not private equity funds) will be exempt from the registration requirement. The Dodd-Frank Act also raises the asset threshold for SEC registration from $25 million to $100 million. Smaller advisers will generally register with the states, although SEC registration is required if an adviser's home state does not regulate advisers or if an adviser is registered to do business in more than 15 states.

Executive Compensation and Corporate Governance

Policy Issues[44]

The financial crisis led to policy concerns about a possible link between excessive financial firm risk taking and executive compensation practices. Beginning in 2008, the Troubled Asset Relief Program subjected recipients to various executive pay restrictions and corporate governance requirements. In the fall of 2009, as part of its safety and soundness regulatory oversight of banks, the Fed proposed to review bank pay structures to identify any compensation arrangements that provide incentives to take excessive.[45] In June 2010, final guidance was issued. These initiatives are significantly premised on the widely held belief that large financial firm incentive pay structures significantly contributed to excessive risk taking. However, at least one major academic study has raised questions concerning the premise.[46]

Provisions in the Dodd-Frank Act (Title IX)

Under the Dodd-Frank Act, at least once every three years, public company shareholders will be able to cast a nonbinding vote to approve executive compensation and where applicable, executive golden parachutes, known generally as "say on pay." The SEC will be permitted to adopt exemptions for small public companies. The act also authorizes the SEC to promulgate rules that would allow shareholders to nominate candidates for a public company's board through the company's proxy materials, a process called proxy access. The SEC may exempt small companies from these provisions.

The Dodd-Frank Act also requires the SEC to amend its rules to require additional disclosure on the relationship between executive compensation and corporate financial performance with respect to such metrics as changes in the value of an issuer's stock and dividend distributions. The SEC must issue rules prohibiting stock exchanges from listing the stock of any company that does not adopt an executive incentive pay "clawback" policy. Specifically, when there is an accounting restatement from material noncompliance with federal financial disclosure laws, a company is required to recover incentive-based compensation awarded to current or former executives based on the erroneous disclosures during three years preceding the restatement.

The Dodd-Frank Act also directs federal financial regulators to jointly adopt guidance requiring applicable financial institutions (including depository institutions, broker-dealers, credit unions, investment advisers, Fannie Mae, and Freddie Mac) with more than $1 billion in assets to prohibit incentive-based pay arrangements for executives, employees, directors, or principal shareholders deemed to be excessive, or that could lead to material financial loss at the financial institution.

Insurance[47]

Policy Issues

Under the McCarran-Ferguson Act of 1945,[48] insurance regulation is generally left to the individual states. For several years prior to the financial crisis, some Members of Congress have introduced legislation to federalize insurance regulation along the lines of the dual regulation of the banking sector, although none of this legislation has reached the committee markup stage.[49]

The financial crisis, particularly the involvement of insurance giant AIG and the smaller monoline bond insurers, changed the tenor of the debate around insurance regulation, with increased emphasis on the systemic importance of some insurance companies. Although it could be argued that insurer involvement in the financial crisis demonstrated the need for full-scale federal regulation of insurance, the financial regulatory reform proposals in the 111th Congress generally have not included language implementing such a system. Instead, such proposals have tended to include the creation of a somewhat narrower federal office focusing on gathering information on insurance and setting policy on international insurance issues. Provisions on consumer protection, investor protection, and systemic risk provisions also have the potential to affect insurance, though insurance has been largely exempted from these aspects of the legislation as well.

Provisions in the Dodd-Frank Act (Title V)

The Dodd-Frank Act creates a new Federal Insurance Office within the Treasury Department. In addition to gathering information and advising on insurance issues, this office would have limited preemptive power over state insurance laws and regulations. This preemption is limited to cases in which the state measures result in less favorable treatment of non-U.S. insurers and in which the case is covered by an existing international agreement. Insurers are exempted from oversight by the act's new Bureau of Consumer Financial Protection. Under the act, systemically significant insurers could be subject to identification by the Financial Stability Oversight Council, regulation by the Federal Reserve and resolution by the special authority created by the act, although resolution of state-chartered insurance companies would continue to occur under the state insurer insolvency regimes. In addition, the Dodd-Frank Act streamlines the state regulation of surplus lines insurance and reinsurance.[50]

Miscellaneous Provisions in the Dodd-Frank Act

The Dodd-Frank Act contains several miscellaneous provisions in various titles of the legislation, including the following:

- *Section 1075: Interchange Fees.* This section authorizes the Federal Reserve to prescribe regulations regarding interchange transaction fees with respect to electronic debit transactions. The amount of such interchange fees must be reasonable and proportional to the costs incurred by the debit card issuer in the transaction. This provision applies to all banks that have $10 billion or more in assets.

- *Title III, Subtitle C: Federal Deposit Insurance Corporation.* This subtitle reforms deposit insurance by altering the assessment base, placing a floor on reserve ratios, and permanently increasing the insured deposit limit to $250,000.
- *Title XII: Improving Access to Mainstream Financial Institutions.* This title includes provisions to expand access to the banking system for families with low and moderate incomes by (1) authorizing a program to help such individuals open low-cost checking or savings accounts at banks or credit unions; and (2) creating a pool of capital to enable community development financial institutions to provide small, local, retail loan programs as alternatives to "pay day" or automobile title loans in local communities.
- *Title XIII: The TARP Pay it Back Act.* This title reduces the amount authorized to be outstanding under the TARP to $475 billion; it was originally $700 billion. It will also prohibit the Treasury from using repaid TARP funds to make new TARP investments.
- *Title XV: Miscellaneous Provisions.* This title requires the Administration to assess proposed loans by the International Monetary Fund to middle-income nations. If it determines that the loan recipient's public debt exceeds its annual gross domestic product, it will have to oppose the loan unless it can certify to Congress that the loan is likely to be repaid. The act also stipulates that entities responsible for production processes or manufactured output that depend on minerals originating in the Democratic Republic of Congo and adjoining countries will be required to provide disclosures to the SEC on the measures taken to exercise due diligence with respect to the source and chain of custody of the materials, and products manufactured from them. In addition, companies will be required to disclose (1) payments to foreign governments for mineral extraction rights, and (2) information regarding mine safety violations.

End Notes

[1] Initially incorporated bills included H.R. 2609, H.R. 3126, H.R. 3269, H.R. 3817, H.R. 3818, H.R. 3890, and H.R. 3996.

[2] The Restoring American Financial Stability Act of 2009 committee print is available at http://banking.senate.gov/ public/_files/111609FullBillTextofTheRestoringAmericanFinancialStabilityActof2009.pdf.

[3] The Restoring American Financial Stability Act of 2010 committee print is available at http://banking.senate.gov/ public/_files/ChairmansMark31510AYO10306_xmlFinancialReformLegislationBill.pdf. The amendment adopted in committee is available at http://banking.senate.gov/public/_files /032310Mangers Amendment AYO10627.pdf.

[4] See http://republicans.financialservices.house.gov/index.php?option=com_content&task= view &id= 601& Itemid=42.

[5] "Blueprint for a Modernized Financial Regulatory Structure" U.S. Treasury, available at http://www.treas.gov/press/ releases/reports/Blueprint.pdf.

[6] Treasury has created websites to track financial intervention and financial reform. See http://ustreas.gov/initiatives/ regulatoryreform/ and http://www.financialstability.gov.

[7] See, for example, "The Panic of 2008," a speech given by Federal Reserve Governor Kevin Warsh on April 6, 2009, for discussion of aspects of typical financial panics and historical examples, available at http://www.federalreserve.gov/ newsevents/speech/warsh20090406a. htm.

[8] Treasury Secretary Timothy F. Geithner, Written Testimony House Financial Services Committee, Financial Regulatory Reform, September 23, 2009, available at http://www.ustreas.gov/press/releases/tg296.htm.

[9] For more information, see CRS Report R40877, *Financial Regulatory Reform: Systemic Risk and the Federal Reserve*, by Marc Labonte.

[10] For an overview of systemic risk, see CRS Report R40417, *Macroprudential Oversight: Monitoring Systemic Risk in the Financial System*, by Darryl E. Getter.

[11] For more information, see CRS Report R41298, *The "Volcker Rule:" Proposals to Limit "Speculative" Proprietary Trading by Banks*, by David H. Carpenter and M. Maureen Murphy.

[12] See CRS Report RL34427, *Financial Turmoil: Federal Reserve Policy Responses*, by Marc Labonte.

[13] 12 U.S.C. § 343.

[14] See CRS Report R40530, *Insolvency of Systemically Significant Financial Companies (SSFCs): Bankruptcy vs. Conservatorship/Receivership*, by David H. Carpenter.

[15] 12 U.S.C. § 1823(c)(4).

[16] For a more in-depth analysis of these resolution regimes, see CRS Report R40530, *Insolvency of Systemically Significant Financial Companies (SSFCs): Bankruptcy vs. Conservatorship/Receivership*, by David H. Carpenter and CRS Report R40928, *Lehman Brothers and IndyMac: Comparing Resolution Regimes*, by David H. Carpenter.

[17] Dodd-Frank Act § 203.

[18] Dodd-Frank Act § 204.

[19] Dodd-Frank Act § 214.

[20] See CRS Report RS22722, *Securitization and Federal Regulation of Mortgages for Safety and Soundness*, by Edward V. Murphy.

[21] See CRS Report R41176, *Federal Financial Services Regulatory Consolidation: Structural Response to the 2007-2009 Financial Crisis*, by Walter W. Eubanks and CRS Report R40249, *Who Regulates Whom? An Overview of U.S. Financial Supervision*, by Mark Jickling and Edward V. Murphy.

[22] See CRS Report R41338, *The Dodd-Frank Wall Street Reform and Consumer Protection Act: Title X, The Consumer Financial Protection Bureau*, by David H. Carpenter.

[23] 15 U.S.C. §§ 1601 *et seq.*

[24] U.S. Department of the Treasury, *Financial Regulatory Reform: A New Foundation*, June 2009, pg. 56, available at http://www.financialstability.gov/docs/regs/FinalReport_web

[25] Dodd-Frank Act § 1024.

[26] Dodd-Frank Act § 1024.

[27] Dodd-Frank Act § 1027(a).

[28] The Dodd-Frank Act streamlines the FTC's rulemaking procedures for declaring trade practices to be unfair or deceptive under the FTC Act, but only with regards to auto dealers. Dodd-Frank Act § 1029. The FTC's general rulemaking procedures under the FTC Act are not altered by the Dodd-Frank Act. 15 U.S.C. § 57a.

[29] See CRS Report RL33775, *Alternative Mortgages: Causes and Policy Implications of Troubled Mortgage Resets in the Subprime and Alt-A Markets*, by Edward V. Murphy.

[30] For more information, see CRS Report R40965, *Key Issues in Derivatives Reform*, by Rena S. Miller.

[31] P.L. 106-554, 114 Stat. 2763.

[32] Dodd-Frank Act § 723 (swaps) and § 763 (security-based swaps (SBS).

[33] Contracts with a large number of underlying securities will be swaps; contracts based on single securities or narrow-based security indexes will be security-based swaps.

[34] Dodd-Frank Act § 723 (Swaps) and § 763 (SBS).

[35] Financial entities are defined, for the purposes of these subsections, as swap dealers, security-based swap dealers, major swap participants, major security-based swap participants, commodity pools, private funds, employee benefit plans, and persons predominantly engaged in activities that are in the business of banking or are financial in nature. The CFTC and SEC are given the power to exempt small banks, savings associations, farm credit system institutions, and credit unions from the definition of financial entities. § 723 (Swaps) and § 763 (SBS) of the Dodd-Frank Act.

[36] Dodd-Frank Act § 716.

[37] See CRS Report R40613, *Credit Rating Agencies and Their Regulation*, by Gary Shorter and Michael V. Seitzinger.

[38] See CRS Report RS22519, *Credit Rating Agency Reform Act of 2006*, by Michael V. Seitzinger.

[39] As an example, federally-insured thrifts were prohibited from owning bonds rated below investment grade by an NRSRO.

[40] Dodd-Frank Act § 991.

[41] See CRS Report RS22482, *Section 404 of the Sarbanes-Oxley Act of 2002 (Management Assessment of Internal Controls): Current Regulation and Congressional Concerns*, by Michael V. Seitzinger.

[42] See CRS Report R40783, *Hedge Funds: Legal History and the Dodd-Frank Act*, by Kathleen Ann Ruane and Michael V. Seitzinger and CRS Report R40783, *Hedge Funds: Legal History and the Dodd-Frank Act*, by Kathleen Ann Ruane and Michael V. Seitzinger.

[43] 15 U.S.C. § 80b-1 *et seq.*

[44] See CRS Report RS22583, *Executive Compensation: SEC Regulations and Congressional Proposals*, by Michael V. Seitzinger.

[45] See CRS Report R40540, *Executive Compensation Limits in Selected Federal Laws*, by Michael V. Seitzinger and Carol A. Pettit.

[46] Rudiger Fahlenbrach, Rene Stulz, and Rene M. Bank, "CEO Incentives and the Credit Crisis," *Charles A. Dice Center Working Paper No. 2009-13*, July 27, 2009, available at SSRN: http://ssrn.com/abstract=1439859.

[47] See CRS Report R41018, *Insurance and Financial Regulatory Reform in the 111th Congress*, by Baird Webel.

[48] 15 U.S.C. § 1011 *et seq.*

[49] See CRS Report R40771, *Insurance Regulation: Issues, Background, and Legislation in the 111th Congress*, by Baird Webel.

[50] See CRS Report RS22506, *Surplus Lines Insurance: Background and Current Legislation*, by Baird Webel.

INDEX

A

access, 12, 47, 107, 110, 136, 139, 142, 144
accountability, 137, 138
accounting, 138, 140, 142
acquisitions, 81, 82
adjustment, 110, 114
Administrative Procedure Act, 3, 6, 75
advancement, 108
adverse effects, 105, 106, 110, 125
agencies, vii, ix, 1, 2, 3, 4, 5, 6, 10, 11, 12, 13, 14, 15, 17, 19, 21, 23, 24, 25, 27, 29, 30, 31, 32, 64, 66, 82, 104, 105, 106, 107, 118, 122, 129, 136, 137, 138
amortization, 133
antitrust, 96, 116
APA, 3, 6, 9, 10, 14, 75, 78, 105, 106
appropriations, 139
Appropriations Act, 5
arbitrage, 129
assessment, 13, 14, 16, 18, 19, 42, 75, 106, 130, 144
audit, 7, 69, 124, 140
authority(s), viii, ix, 8, 9, 10, 34, 41, 57, 66, 81, 82, 96, 98, 105, 106, 109, 118, 122, 123, 124, 126, 127, 129, 131, 132, 133, 136, 138, 139, 143

B

balance sheet, 36, 40, 43, 46, 47, 54, 85, 91, 109, 110, 123, 126, 127, 133
bank holding companies, 3, 7, 9, 32, 33, 34, 35, 38, 40, 41, 42, 43, 46, 50, 53, 55, 67, 68, 79, 80, 81, 82, 83, 84, 86, 87, 88, 90, 91, 92, 105, 107, 108, 109, 110, 113, 123, 126
bankers, 120
banking, 5, 8, 23, 27, 29, 30, 31, 35, 43, 82, 85, 86, 97, 107, 108, 109, 113, 123, 126, 127, 129, 130, 132, 139, 142, 144, 145, 146
banking industry, 8
banking sector, 142
bankruptcy(s), 104, 120, 124, 126
base, 84, 100, 106, 116, 119, 130, 136, 144, 146
basis points, 56, 93, 116
benefits, 2, 5, 12, 13, 14, 15, 17, 18, 19, 20, 21, 22, 70, 71, 72, 73, 74, 75, 95, 106, 140
board members, 140
bonds, 137, 146
borrowers, 124, 127, 128, 133, 134, 135
breakdown, 122
business model, 86
businesses, 34, 105, 126, 128, 133
buyer(s), 120, 127

C

candidates, 142
capital adequacy, 54, 68, 84, 85, 88, 91, 92
capital markets, 58, 86
capital standards, viii, 118
case studies, vii, 1, 6
cash, 47, 80, 85, 96, 109, 110, 115
cash flow, 80, 109
central bank, 120
challenges, 23
City, 114, 115
classes, viii, 13, 71, 118, 128
clients, 140, 141
collaboration, 32, 64
collateral, 112, 121, 135
commercial, 8, 58, 68, 87, 88, 101, 123, 128, 129, 136
commercial bank, 8, 68, 88, 101, 123, 129, 136
commodity, 135, 146
commodity futures, 135
community(s), 144
compensation, ix, 59, 60, 63, 69, 81, 112, 113, 118, 125, 126, 134, 139, 141, 142
compensation package, 60
competition, 13, 57, 93, 96, 98, 105, 106, 110, 129, 134
competitiveness, 12, 97
complexity, 34, 35, 36, 40, 41, 42, 43, 68, 79, 108, 127
compliance, 30, 106, 116, 130
conference, viii, 29, 118, 119
configuration, 8
conflict, 6, 30, 67, 130, 137
conflict of interest, 137
Congo, 144
Congress, viii, 4, 19, 115, 117, 119, 121, 124, 139, 142, 143, 144, 147
consensus, 28, 30
consent, 112
consolidation, 112, 129
consulting, 69, 113
consumer choice, 134
consumer protection, viii, 4, 55, 69, 118, 130, 131, 132, 143
Consumer Protection Act, v, viii, 2, 4, 25, 55, 70, 71, 77, 108, 117, 118, 119, 146
consumers, 12, 13, 21, 22, 92, 96, 104, 114, 121, 122, 126, 128, 131, 132, 134
consumption, 121
contingency, 47, 80, 109
control group, 83, 100
conversations, 28
coordination, 3, 6, 22, 23, 24, 25, 26, 27, 28, 29, 30, 31, 32, 64, 66, 107
corporate governance, 60, 69, 141
cost, 2, 5, 7, 12, 13, 14, 15, 17, 18, 21, 30, 50, 53, 54, 65, 75, 83, 84, 88, 89, 90, 96, 104, 106, 113, 124, 131, 135, 144
cost saving, 96
cost-benefit analysis, 21, 104
costs of compliance, 104
counseling, 135
credit rating, ix, 55, 58, 118, 127, 137, 138
Credit Rating Agency Reform Act, 146
creditors, 85, 125
creditworthiness, 121, 137
crises, 120, 122
customers, 96, 97, 99, 115, 116, 139

D

damages, 125
danger, 125
data availability, 68
data collection, 3, 65
data processing, 131
database, 65
DCI, 3, 65, 66
debts, 47
decision makers, 5
deflator, 68
delinquency, 133
Democratic Republic of Congo, 144
Department of Defense, 5
Department of Justice, 96, 111, 116
Department of Labor, 26
Department of the Treasury, 6, 26, 66, 146

dependent variable, 84, 100, 101
deposit accounts, 97, 101, 102, 103, 111, 115
depository institutions, viii, 8, 12, 29, 82, 85, 107, 108, 110, 118, 122, 125, 130, 131, 132, 136, 142
deposits, 9, 84, 85, 107, 110, 115, 124
depth, 6, 24, 65, 67, 145
derivatives, viii, 47, 85, 110, 118, 121, 135
direct cost(s), 18, 19
directors, 59, 60, 105, 124, 142
disbursement, 115
disclosure, ix, 58, 59, 112, 118, 124, 137, 139, 142
dislocation, 109
disposition, 112
distress, 34, 36, 41, 109, 120
distribution, 19
diversification, 40
Dodd-Frank Wall Street Reform and Consumer Protection Act, viii, 2, 4, 55, 70, 71, 77, 108, 118, 119, 146
draft, 2, 10, 20, 31, 64

E

earnings, 54, 68, 84, 85, 91, 92
economic activity, 34
economic consequences, 21, 109
economic downturn, 35
economic growth, 50
economies of scale, 19, 40
electronic banking, 13
e-mail, 28
emergency, ix, 118, 123, 124
employees, 142
employment, 105, 106, 110
enforcement, 8, 16, 58, 123, 129, 130, 131, 133
engineering, 140
equipment, 58, 62, 98, 111, 112
equity, 36, 43, 46, 48, 49, 50, 53, 59, 81, 85, 88, 89, 90, 107, 109, 112, 113, 123, 130, 136, 140, 141
equity market, 113
Europe, 87
European Commission, 29
European Union, 30
evidence, 5, 7, 24, 69, 105
examinations, 104, 105
exclusion, 110
executive order(s), 2, 3, 5, 12, 13, 106
exercise, 20, 78, 82, 144
expertise, 8
exposure, 36, 43, 46, 53, 80, 87, 90, 121, 123
extraction, 144

F

families, 144
Fannie Mae, 112, 120, 128, 142
federal agencies, vii, 1, 4, 6, 12, 13, 23, 32, 104, 105, 106, 107
federal assistance, 136
federal banking regulators, 43, 139
federal funds, 85, 110
federal government, 4, 9
Federal Housing Finance Agency (FHFA), 107, 128
federal law, 130, 137
federal office, ix, 118, 143
Federal Register, 10, 16, 24, 27, 29, 65, 67, 75, 78, 82, 104, 107
Federal Reserve Board, 16, 36, 64, 68, 74, 88, 125
federal support, viii, 117
financial condition, viii, 117
financial crisis, 4, 23, 33, 41, 43, 46, 121, 125, 133, 134, 140, 141, 142, 143
financial data, 131
financial distress, 33, 34, 81
financial firms, viii, 34, 41, 67, 118, 120, 121, 123, 124, 133, 137
financial innovation, 134
financial instability, 42, 108
financial institutions, 4, 7, 13, 33, 36, 40, 41, 59, 67, 80, 82, 105, 107, 119, 121, 125, 126, 131, 142, 144
financial markets, 4, 65, 119, 120, 122, 140

financial performance, 142
financial regulation, ix, 8, 104, 118
financial resources, 128
financial sector, 82, 109, 127
Financial Services Authority, 29
financial services regulations, vii, 1, 5
financial shocks, 130
financial stability, 8, 11, 34, 41, 50, 64, 79, 81, 82, 108, 109, 125, 126, 134
financial system, viii, 4, 9, 23, 33, 34, 40, 50, 67, 81, 108, 109, 117, 118, 120, 121, 122, 125, 132, 134
foreclosure, 132, 133
formation, 8, 13
formula, 130
fragility, viii, 118
fraud, 8, 56, 93, 110, 112, 114
Freddie Mac, 112, 120, 128, 142
FSB, 4, 42, 83, 109
fund transfers, 13
funding, 3, 47, 54, 68, 80, 84, 86, 88, 91, 92, 109, 113, 126, 127, 138, 139
funds, ix, 34, 46, 84, 85, 92, 107, 110, 115, 118, 121, 123, 126, 140, 141, 144, 146

G

GAO, vii, ix, 1, 2, 3, 5, 7, 9, 16, 27, 29, 36, 37, 38, 39, 44, 45, 48, 49, 51, 52, 53, 63, 64, 65, 66, 68, 69, 75, 78, 90, 96, 103, 104, 105, 106, 107, 111, 114, 118, 124
GDP, 4, 68
global economy, 34
governance, 141
governments, 9, 32, 144
grades, 137
grading, 137
Great Depression, 120, 121
greed, 119
gross domestic product, 4, 68, 144
growth, 40, 59, 81, 85, 108, 123
guidance, 2, 6, 11, 12, 13, 15, 17, 18, 20, 21, 22, 31, 32, 64, 75, 105, 106, 107, 108, 132, 141, 142

H

harmonization, 30
health, 59
hedging, 128
height, 59
historical data, 60
history, 7, 34, 58, 67
holding company, 35, 36, 39, 42, 43, 48, 49, 51, 52, 53, 54, 80, 81, 84, 85, 86, 87, 88, 90, 91, 108, 113, 129, 130
homeowners, 133
homes, 121, 133
House, viii, 117, 119, 120, 145
housing, 121, 126, 134, 135, 137
Housing and Urban Development, 107, 128
housing boom, 137
HUD, 128
human, 19
human behavior, 19

I

identification, 4, 13, 21, 57, 92, 111, 143
illiquid asset, 124
impact assessment, 18
improvements, 46, 54, 91, 106
income, 13, 47, 53, 56, 85, 86, 89, 90, 94, 95, 97, 100, 101, 102, 103, 104, 116, 128, 133, 134, 144
income tax, 133
independence, 64, 129
independent variable, 84, 86, 100, 101
individuals, 140, 144
industry(s), vii, 1, 4, 8, 18, 22, 28, 32, 33, 40, 41, 56, 93, 95, 140
inflation, 38, 61, 62, 112
infrastructure, 34
initiation, 10, 28
integrity, 8, 12, 20, 137, 138, 139
interagency coordination, vii, 1, 2, 3, 6, 22, 23, 24, 28, 30, 31, 32, 67, 107
interagency relationships, 31
interest rates, 133, 136

internal controls, 124
Internal Revenue Service, 26
International Monetary Fund, 144
intervention, 145
investment(s), viii, ix, 58, 85, 86, 105, 106, 110, 117, 118, 121, 123, 138, 139, 140, 141, 142, 144, 146
investment bank, viii, 86, 117
investors, ix, 8, 13, 21, 58, 59, 60, 69, 118, 122, 127, 128, 137, 138, 139, 140
issue-by-issue basis, viii, 117
issues, ix, 10, 28, 31, 32, 105, 107, 118, 119, 139, 143

J

jurisdiction, 8, 22, 30, 122, 132

L

laws, 8, 112, 130, 131, 132, 137, 142, 143
laws and regulations, 130, 131, 137, 143
lead, 41, 42, 50, 95, 97, 129, 142
legislation, viii, 8, 117, 119, 121, 124, 130, 134, 135, 142, 143
lending, 50, 112, 121, 123, 124, 127, 134
light, 12, 14, 130
limited liability, 124
liquid assets, 36, 47, 52, 54, 85, 91, 92, 110
liquidity, 3, 34, 35, 42, 46, 47, 50, 54, 68, 79, 80, 84, 85, 86, 91, 92, 108, 109, 110, 120, 121, 122, 123, 127, 137, 140
liquidity ratio, 55, 80, 91
loans, 46, 59, 84, 86, 87, 94, 112, 123, 124, 126, 128, 132, 133, 134, 135, 144

M

magnitude, 18
major issues, 28
majority, 14, 60, 113, 140
management, 10, 12, 18, 28, 31, 50, 80, 85, 124, 125, 141
manipulation, 8
manufactured housing, 62, 112
market discipline, 8, 40
market share, 35, 39, 41, 111, 116
marketing, 138
marketplace, 5, 7, 8, 33, 67, 104, 139
materials, 142, 144
matter, 8
median, 35, 36, 39, 41, 42, 46, 47, 48, 49, 51, 52, 113
membership, 140
mergers, 82
methodology, 7, 19, 53, 108
mission, 8, 64
monetary policy, 35, 129
moral hazard, 41, 109
moratorium, 130
mortgage-backed securities, 87, 112, 127, 137

N

negative effects, 133
neutral, 63, 112
New York Stock Exchange, 140

O

Obama, viii, 118, 119, 131
Obama Administration, 119, 131
Obama, President, viii, 118
Office of Management and Budget, 2, 4, 5, 65
Office of the Comptroller of the Currency (OCC), viii, 7, 118
Office of Thrift Supervision (OTS), viii, 118, 129
officials, 7, 66, 67, 69, 108
OMB, 2, 4, 5, 6, 12, 13, 15, 17, 18, 19, 21, 64, 65, 104, 105, 106, 110
opacity, 121, 135
open market operations, 124
operations, 40, 41, 80, 81, 108, 124, 131
opportunities, 10
organize, 5
outreach, 113

overlap, 2, 22, 139
oversight, ix, 4, 8, 33, 34, 50, 67, 68, 84, 118, 123, 129, 138, 141, 143
ownership, 81
ownership structure, 81

P

participants, viii, 7, 8, 12, 18, 19, 20, 21, 30, 40, 55, 69, 118, 121, 135, 136, 146
peer group, 113
penalties, 133, 134
permit, 80, 138
platform, 114
policy, 6, 10, 31, 32, 75, 78, 104, 109, 120, 121, 125, 129, 130, 141, 142, 143
policy options, 121, 125
policymakers, 125, 129, 135
pools, 146
potential benefits, 12, 15, 17, 19, 22, 110
President, viii, 118, 125
President Obama, viii, 118
prevention, 56, 93, 110, 114
principles, 6, 65, 106
private sector, 125
probability, 50
professionals, 113
profit, 105, 130
project, 80, 109
proposed regulations, 7, 47, 108, 109
proprietary trading activities, 123
protection, viii, 12, 13, 20, 85, 107, 112, 118, 130, 131, 132, 143
prudential regulation, viii, 3, 7, 87, 118
Public Company Accounting Oversight Board, 70
public concern, 12
public debt, 144
public interest, 10, 12, 13, 14
public policy, 9
public resources, 124

R

rating agencies, ix, 118, 137
reactions, 34, 92
real estate, viii, 85, 117, 131, 133
real time, 17
reasoning, 19
recession, 55, 91, 121
recommendations, 2, 82, 83, 139
recovery, 55, 91
recurrence, 120
reform(s), v, vii, viii, ix, 1, 2, 4, 25, 33, 43, 46, 50, 55, 67, 70, 71, 77, 108, 109, 117, 118, 119, 120, 121, 135, 138, 143, 144, 145, 146, 147
regression, 3, 7, 50, 56, 68, 84, 100, 111
regression analysis, 3, 7, 50, 56, 68, 111
regulations, vii, 1, 2, 3, 4, 5, 7, 8, 10, 11, 14, 15, 17, 18, 22, 23, 24, 33, 55, 58, 65, 66, 67, 69, 81, 91, 104, 109, 129, 130, 131, 132, 134, 137, 138, 139, 143
regulatory agencies, 2, 5, 8, 10, 12, 14, 104, 105, 106, 122, 138
regulatory analyses, vii, 1, 2, 5, 11, 14, 65, 105
regulatory oversight, 19, 141
reinsurance, 143
reliability, 69, 140
relief, 132
remediation, 79, 81
resilience, 33, 34, 35, 36, 67
resolution, viii, 34, 41, 81, 83, 108, 109, 110, 118, 124, 125, 126, 143, 145
resources, 10, 31, 124, 128, 138
response, 4, 14, 35, 57, 64, 99, 111, 116, 121
restaurants, 96
restitution, 125
restrictions, viii, 8, 16, 40, 81, 82, 95, 96, 108, 118, 135, 141
retail, ix, 97, 118, 139, 144
retirement, 121
revenue, 18, 86, 87, 93, 97, 99, 111
rewards, 115
rights, 125, 138, 144

risk(s), ix, 8, 12, 19, 20, 23, 27, 28, 29, 30, 31, 34, 36, 40, 43, 46, 49, 50, 53, 64, 79, 80, 81, 82, 85, 88, 89, 90, 108, 109, 118, 120, 121, 122, 124, 126, 127, 128, 131, 132, 135, 136, 137, 140, 141, 143, 145
risk management, 19, 47, 80, 81, 82, 109, 124
roots, 121
rural areas, 12

S

safety, 3, 7, 33, 50, 54, 68, 83, 84, 91, 104, 120, 123, 129, 130, 132, 141, 144
sanctions, 16
Sarbanes-Oxley Act, 140, 146
savings, 9, 56, 68, 88, 94, 95, 96, 97, 101, 104, 111, 115, 120, 121, 144, 146
savings account, 115, 121, 144
savings banks, 9, 68, 88, 94, 101
SCAP, 4
scope, 6, 7, 14, 31, 55, 65, 66, 69, 75, 91, 106
Secretary of the Treasury, 9, 107, 125
security(s), 3, 5, 8, 11, 16, 17, 30, 58, 69, 71, 85, 87, 105, 110, 111, 112, 121, 126, 127, 128, 135, 136, 137, 138, 139, 140, 146
Securities Act of 1933, 58
Securities Exchange Act, 13, 59
self-regulation, 8
seller(s), 133
Senate, viii, 117, 119
service provider, 139
services, vii, 1, 4, 5, 8, 12, 13, 18, 33, 34, 35, 40, 43, 69, 96, 97, 111, 131, 132, 133, 139
shareholders, 59, 60, 113, 125, 142
shock, 120, 121, 128
short-term liabilities, 36, 47, 51, 52, 110
showing, 65
skin, 127
small businesses, 133
speech, 145
spillover effects, 35, 36
spin, 120
stability, 9, 33, 34, 50, 81, 82, 120, 121, 125, 126, 132, 134, 135
standard error, 90, 103
state(s), 8, 9, 13, 19, 65, 97, 105, 106, 112, 113, 116, 123, 126, 129, 130, 137, 140, 141, 142, 143
state regulators, 8
statutes, 2, 6, 11, 12, 13, 14, 65, 69, 105, 137, 138
statutory authority, 6
stock, 80, 109, 142
stock exchange, 142
stress, 41, 43, 47, 50, 79, 80, 81, 83, 85, 92, 109, 123
stress test, 43, 47, 50, 79, 80, 81, 83, 92, 109, 123
stress testing, 109
structure, 8, 41, 57, 95, 99, 111, 114, 115, 116
substitutes, 43
supervision, 9, 11, 32, 34, 41, 47, 67, 79, 81, 105, 107, 108, 110, 129, 130, 131
supervisor, 131, 132
Supervisory Capital Assessment Program (SCAP), 4, 81
surplus, 80, 143
Switzerland, 109, 110
systemic risk, vii, 1, 3, 8, 40, 81, 120, 122, 124, 131, 141, 143, 145

T

teams, 21
technical assistance, 21
technical comments, 2, 64
telephone, 28
telephone conversations, 28
threats, 9, 34
thrifts, 8, 9, 129, 130, 146
time deposits, 85, 110
time frame, 41
Title I, 25, 32, 41, 70, 81, 125, 127, 129, 137, 139, 141, 142, 144
Title II, 25, 32, 41, 70, 81, 125, 129, 144

Title IV, 141
Title V, 23, 130, 143
tracks, 40, 65
trade, 5, 136, 146
trade-off, 5
tranches, 128
transaction value, 56, 94, 95, 96, 113, 115
transactions, 8, 16, 34, 56, 57, 58, 85, 93, 95, 96, 97, 98, 99, 110, 111, 112, 114, 115, 116, 139, 143
transparency, 20, 41, 122, 136
Treasury, viii, 6, 14, 16, 18, 19, 20, 27, 64, 66, 74, 75, 77, 105, 107, 108, 117, 118, 119, 120, 122, 124, 125, 126, 139, 143, 144, 145
Treasury Secretary, viii, 117, 118, 119, 120, 122, 124, 145
treatment, 83, 84, 88, 91, 100, 103, 143
trial, 105
triggers, 81

U

U.S. Department of the Treasury, 146
U.S. Treasury, 145
underwriting, 58, 86, 127, 128
unions, 8, 9, 94, 101, 112, 129, 130, 142, 144, 146
United, v, 1, 8, 11, 34, 36, 42, 47, 81, 82, 93, 113, 114, 124, 125, 128, 130, 132, 133
United States, v, 1, 8, 11, 34, 36, 42, 47, 81, 82, 93, 113, 114, 124, 125, 128, 130, 132, 133
USA, 114

V

variables, 53, 85, 86, 90
variations, 9
vehicles, 127, 140
venture capital, 86, 141
Volcker Rule, 23, 145
vote, 59, 60, 63, 69, 82, 112, 119, 123, 142
voting, 9, 105, 112
vulnerability, 23, 34

W

Wall Street Reform, v, viii, 2, 4, 25, 55, 70, 71, 77, 108, 117, 118, 119, 146
Washington, 83, 104, 105, 108, 109, 114
web, 146
websites, 145
witnesses, 105
writing process, 64

Y

yield, 13